VEGAN SECRET SUPPER

VEGAN SECRET SUPPER

Bold & Elegant Menus from a Rogue Kitchen

MÉRIDA ANDERSON

ARSENAL PULP PRESS
VANCOUVER

VEGAN SECRET SUPPER
Copyright © 2013 by Mérida Anderson

ARSENAL PULP PRESS
Suite 101 – 211 East Georgia St.
Vancouver, BC V6A 1Z6
Canada
arsenalpulp.com

The publisher gratefully acknowledges the support of the Government of Canada (through the Canada Book Fund) and the Government of British Columbia (through the Book Publishing Tax Credit Program) for its publishing activities.

The author and publisher assert that the information contained in this book is true and complete to the best of their knowledge. All recommendations are made without the guarantee on the part of the author and publisher. The author and publisher disclaim any liability in connection with the use of this information. For more information, contact the publisher.

Note for our UK readers: measurements for non-liquids are for volume, not weight.

Design by Lindsey Hampton
Interior photographs by Mérida Anderson
Cover and additional photographs by Danny Rico
Editing by Susan Safyan
Nutritional analysis and research by Zsofia Zambo, MSc, Human Nutrition

Printed and bound in Canada

Library and Archives Canada Cataloguing in Publication:

Anderson, Mérida
       Vegan secret supper : bold & elegant menus from a
rogue kitchen / Mérida Anderson.

Includes index.
Issued also in an electronic format.
ISBN 978-1-55152-496-2

    1. Vegan cooking. 2. Cookbooks. I. Title.

TX837.A455 2013   641.5'636   C2012-906809-8

For Erin Edwards, for being the best server VSS ever had and for bringing me a bow tie so we would match.

For Quori, who took over for Erin, ended up on the East Coast, and continues to serve.

For Alissa Raye, who let me turn our tiny attic in East Vancouver into a restaurant.

For all the ladies at the Green Haus for letting me do the same, and the many folks at 433 who let me take over their entire main floor. And everyone at The Penthouse in Brooklyn for eating all the leftovers.

For Zsofia Zambo, who lets me use her kitchen when I cook in Montreal.

For Peewee, the best host VSS ever had.

And for my mum, who wouldn't cook for me anymore after I told her I was vegan—until she herself became vegetarian. (I had learned to cook by then.)

THANK YOU!

CONTENTS

FOREWORD BY ERIN EDWARDS

I've been friends with Mérida for close to six years now, and I've known her to do a lot of things. When we first met, she was a fashion designer who was apprenticing as a hair-stylist, working on an album, and planning to take a bike-frame welding class, who then opened an art gallery. I knew she was vegan, but I was pretty skeptical when she told me about her Secret Supper idea and asked me to be her first server. At that time, I was one of those rather misinformed people who thought that even if prepared well, vegan food just would never quite "measure up."

I've never had a better time eating my words.

Operating out of a kitchen the size of an average closet, Mérida prepared some of the most memorable meals I've ever had, vegan or not (I still dream about her sweet potato crème brûlée). I would even eat the pot scrapings at the end of the dinner service. But my appreciation for her food wasn't the only indication that Mérida was doing something really amazing; it was plainly obvious whenever I served a beautifully presented meal to guests that they couldn't wait to dig in. And they would always make a point of finding the chef before they left to thank her for the lovely meal.

I especially looked forward to serving at Vegan Secret Supper on Sunday nights—not just because we got to wear matching bow ties and eat the leftovers, but for the entire experience Mérida created, all in her own home. From the music to the perfectly mis-matched chairs and cutlery to the delicate, delicious smells wafting in from the closet-sized kitchen, Mérida just has a way with food.

In fact, I'd say she's damn near visionary. We're all fortunate that Chef M has decided to share the secrets from the Secret Supper kitchen. Mérida's recipes will surpass your every expectation.

Bon appétit!

Second Lieutenant Erin Edwards is a pilot with the Royal Canadian Air Force.

INTRODUCTION

Vegan Secret Supper (VSS) grew from humble beginnings in the fall of 2008. In a kitchen half the size of a walk-in closet in a tiny attic apartment in East Vancouver, my raccoon-cat Peewee and I invited anyone who swooned for a plant-based supper. Every Sunday, we served a three-to-five-course meal with an ever-changing vegan menu of seasonal, homemade foods, right down to the sourdough bread. After just one year, VSS was serving up to forty people each Sunday.

As word spread, so did my passion for cooking. Cooking for people is really the best feeling, especially when the room goes quiet as you serve a course. VSS offered our guests a unique and intimate dining experience, serving vegan fare that you couldn't get anywhere else in Vancouver, and filling an alternative niche for diners who wanted something different, and personal.

Since then, VSS and I have traveled eastward, hosting secret suppers in Montreal and Brooklyn.

Let's get the credentials out of the way. I don't have any culinary schooling. I haven't worked much in restaurants. My cred is 100-percent street. For me, cooking is trial, error, and love. I believe that anyone can do any-

thing that they put their mind to. I have had many successful business ventures in my young life so far—fashion designer, gallery and art space curator, ceramicist, to name a few—and vegan chef. And with all of these endeavors, I just do it and figure it out along the way. It's the same for the collection of menus in this book: VSS is an experience, and these recipes reflect that.

Don't be afraid to experiment with the recipes; consider them starting points for your own interpretations. A lot of the menus in this book can be taken apart and put back together in different ways, with aspects (a side, a sauce, a salad) from one menu replacing those from another. As well, know that most of these recipes make enough for six to eight people and can easily be halved for smaller groups.

Many recipes can be made ahead of time. A typical VSS prep is two to three days for a four-course supper, including soaking nuts, making sauces, and refrigerating some desserts overnight. Have patience, and first read the recipes carefully to determine what needs to be made ahead of time. This is slow food at its best.

ORGANICS

Organic farming is focused on the sustainability of the environment and emphasizes soil fertility, water conservation, and biodiversity. The techniques of organic farmers predate modern technologies by thousands of years and include the use of animal and green fertilizers and crop rotation. Most people know that synthetic chemical pesticides aren't used in organic farming. Pesticides prevent crop damage and destruction from insects, parasites, and fungi. However, the cost of mass-producing blemish-free crops comes at a high price, as pesticides used in conventional food production are toxic and, at high levels of exposure, potentially carcinogenic. Chemical pesticides used in agricultural practices cannot be effectively removed by rinsing produce. The most effective method for removing pesticides is to peel fruits and vegetables, but this often means also removing the most nutrient-dense part of the food. And because some pesticides contain heavy metals (like arsenic, mercury, and cadmium), the pesticides in food are still harmful to us even when cooked.

The benefits of organic farming are numerous, but one of the most important is that this practice produces amazingly flavorful and nutritionally dense foods. I find that the taste of an organic apple, for example, highly surpasses that of conventional. However, organic foods are more expensive than those conventionally grown. For families on a budget, it can be helpful to know which foods are more important to buy organic if a complete organic grocery bag is not either financially possible or available at the local grocery store.

At VSS, I cook with mainly organic ingredients, but if they aren't available, I buy local. It's important to buy certain foods organic or at least pesticide-free, especially when they are going to be eaten raw. These include foods that tend to absorb more pesticides and usually have more porous skins, such as stone fruits (peaches, nectarines, apricots, plums), berries, and leafy greens. Some crops, like apples and potatoes, conventionally utilize more pesticides. Though these have peelable skins, all the nutrients, like vitamin C, are found in potato skins. It's also important to buy organic nuts, because they can absorb high amounts of toxins.

Another significant consideration is buying locally grown foods. The "locally grown" label denotes a geographic boundary within which the food is grown (e.g., 100 miles). The advantages to buying locally grown produce are numerous and include improved freshness and taste, supporting your local economy, and reducing the environmental impacts of shipping foods across vast distances. Sometimes I face a dilemma: Do I buy the organic but flown-in-from-New-Zealand apple or the non-organic apple produced on a farm forty minutes away? Neither option is absolutely and always correct, but educating yourself on where your food comes from and how it is processed is the first step in making responsible food decisions that affect your health and the environment.

ABOUT COOKING VEGETABLES

Cooking makes many foods more digestible, aiding us in utilizing their nutrients and energy, as well as improving their texture and palatability. For example, lightly cooking spinach releases calcium and iron, allowing us to absorb these nutrients. However, over-cooking vegetables destroys heat-sensitive vitamins such as A, B1, C, D, and E. It's best to cook your vegetables for a shorter time at a higher temperature than a longer time at a lower one. Lightly steaming them is often best.

FERMENTATION

The human body contains more bacterial cells than we do human cells. It has been suggested that humans and bacterium co-evolved to create a beneficial relationship for both parties: we give bacteria a place to live, and in return they help to break down our food and protect us from the harmful bacteria. Current research examines the links between a lack of good bacteria in the human digestive system and digestive illnesses such as colitis, irritable bowel syndrome, and celiac disease (an autoimmune disease in which the body mounts an immune response to the proteins found in gluten).

Long before we had electricity for refrigerators to keep our foods cold, bacteria were used to preserve foods. Now we depend less on fermented foods than we used to, and sometimes finding foods with active bacterial culture is a challenge. Adding fermented foods like non-dairy yogurts, raw sauerkraut, and miso to a vegan diet is necessary, as they supply some of the few vegan sources of vitamin B12 (also found in nutritional yeast).

NUTS

I cook with a lot of nuts. They are a great alternative to soy; filling, flavorful, and full of protein, iron, and good fats. When preparing raw nuts in many recipes, mostly desserts, I first soak them overnight. This makes them easier to blend smoothly, as well as making them more digestible. Nuts are best stored refrigerated, which gives them a longer shelf life. In warm weather, soak nuts in the refrigerator to prevent spoilage.

OILS

Choosing a good cooking oil is essential when you decide to get behind the stove and whip up something to eat. The chemical structure of various oils differs, making some better for frying and others better for baking. Poly-unsaturated oils (like olive oil) are not recommended for frying because high temperatures break down the molecular structure of the oil and create free radicals. These destructive molecules can lead to cancer. Fortunately, free-radical fighting antioxidants such as alpha-tocopherol or vitamin E, which is found in vegetable oils, combat free radicals in the body.

It's also important to choose oils that are unrefined or at least processed without chemical solvents to ensure the highest nutritional quality as well as flavor. Cold-pressed oils are a little more expensive, but they preserve the fatty acids and vitamin content naturally found in the oils. Unrefined oils are filtered, but their natural fragrance, flavor, color and, most important, nutrients are intact. Extra virgin olive oil offers the highest quality flavor and nutritional value, and I use it for baking and in salad dressings.

Fry with oils that can handle high temperatures; these tend to be lower in polyunsaturated fatty acids and higher in saturated fatty acids. I prefer to fry with grapeseed oil, but use other vegetable oils too, including safflower, sunflower, and coconut oil. I often use refined coconut oil for frying, as it has few impurities and can withstand a higher heat. The refined oil has a milder coconut flavor, making it more versatile to cook with. Refined coconut oil is used in most of the desserts in this book.

One last point to consider with oil is that, in addition to being heat sensitive, all oils are light sensitive, so store them in dark containers or keep them away from light in the cupboards to improve their shelf life.

FLOURS AND GRAINS

Most of the recipes that use flour in this book specify spelt, with a few exceptions, including sourdough. There are many kinds of spelt flour, but the one called for in this book is white spelt. Spelt is known as an ancient grain because it is an ancestor of common wheat. It's a great option for those who are intolerant of common wheat or wish to eat less of it. A hearty grain with a slightly nutty taste, spelt is high in fiber and acts much like wheat in cooking and baking. Although considered a good wheat-free option, it is not gluten-free and should not be served to those with sensitivities to gluten or celiac disease. Gluten is a protein found in many grains, including wheat, kamut, spelt, rye, and barley. More than half of the recipes in this book are gluten-free, utilizing options such as rice, chickpea, and corn flour.

Despite the growing numbers of people with sensitivities or allergies to gluten, it will never be removed from flour because of its crucial role in the chemistry of bread-making. In baking, the gluten in flour binds with water, adding elasticity to the dough. Gluten gives bread a light and chewy texture. For this reason, I use organic whole wheat flour for my sourdough breads and starters to produce higher rising and less dense bread than spelt can provide. The fermentation process that the flour goes through to make sourdough helps to make the wheat more digestible than that in yeasted breads.

REFINED FOODS

The refinement process, whether of oils, flours, or sugars, decreases the nutritional value of foods while creating more homogeneous, "consumer-friendly" products. Refined white flour has been bleached and its health-promoting fibers, vitamins, and minerals removed. Although foods that undergo refinement are usually fortified with (often synthetic) nutrient replacements, they may be lacking the potential health benefits of whole foods, which contain components that haven't been replaced, such as phytochemicals, antioxidants, and trace minerals.

SUGARS AND SWEETENERS

I tend to use liquid sweeteners in my recipes—mostly maple syrup, brown rice syrup, and agave nectar. Maple syrup is the sweetest of the three and has a strong flavor. Use organic maple syrup, as conventionally grown may use animal (bone) char in the refinement process. Brown rice syrup, made from fermented brown rice, is thick and mildly sweet with a complex palate. made from fermented brown rice. Agave nectar, made from the agave cactus, is mild in flavor, slightly less expensive than maple syrup, and can be used in its place. Agave nectar is also used in raw cuisine and has a low glycemic index.

Another sweetener I use a lot in baking is Medjool dates, sometimes known as "the king" or "the diamond" of dates. These are large caramel-colored dates, plump, chewy, and very sweet, and not to be confused with California dried cooking dates, available in the baking section of most grocery stores; these are an inferior but acceptable substitute for Medjool dates, in a pinch.

MILK ALTERNATIVES

There are many milk alternatives available today; the best known is made from soy. Most of the recipes in this book can be made with any nondairy milk of your choice. When soy milk is specifically called for, the recipe results may be different if you substitute another milk for it.

These recipes also use a lot of coconut milk, especially in the desserts. The higher the quality of the coconut milk, the better the results. Use coconut milk with the highest fat content and avoid light (i.e., low-fat) coconut milks, especially when making desserts where thickening and setting will be affected.

SOY

When my friends and I were young vegetarians, we got so excited when they started to sell tofu at our local grocery store, and we were absolutely over-the-moon when chocolate soy milk finally came out. However, the novelty of soy has worn off, and it even takes a bit of work to avoid it in most vegetarian/vegan products, as well as in everyday processed foods. Tofu and processed foods made with soy, like faux meats and dairy, can be hard to digest, and because it is found in so many products, there are more people discovering soy allergies. Tofu is also a cliché of vegan cooking, with negative connotations; the over-use of tofu in meatless cooking is precisely why this cookbook does not contain much of it.

A couple of recipes do feature soy products, including tempeh, which is fermented soy; it is more digestible than tofu and its nutrient content can more easily be absorbed. Tamari soy sauce also appears a lot in this book. Tamari is slightly thicker and has a richer taste than regular soy sauce. It tends to be smoother and less salty, too. During fermentation, it requires less wheat than soy sauce. I use a gluten-free tamari.

With a whole foods approach to cooking, you can utilize the texture, nutrition, and flavors of various vegetables, legumes, nuts, and grains available at the average grocery store. There are more creative ways to be vegan than throwing tofu into a frying pan, and it is time that vegan cooking evolved from being "food without meat or dairy" to what it really is or can be: delicious—even decadent—rich, and versatile cuisine, free of animal products and processed ingredients.

STARTERS

- PEPPER-CRUSTED CASHEW CHEESE PLATE WITH JUNIPER TOFU & OLIVE TAPENADE
- BAKED EGGPLANT SAMOSAS WITH ASSORTED CHUTNEYS & COCONUT SOUR CREAM
- CRISPY OYSTER MUSHROOM, SQUASH BLOSSOM & SWEET POTATO TEMPURA WITH GINGER MISO SAUCE & SESAME SWEET RICE
- BRAZIL NUT SEA PÂTÉ WITH APPLES & SPRING ONIONS
- APPLE-SMOKED TOFU & CARAMELIZED ONION SPRING ROLLS WITH CARROT TAMARIND CHUTNEY & AVOCADO AIOLI
- SEASONAL SQUASH & HEIRLOOM TOMATOES TOSSED WITH PEAR WALNUT BUTTER, SERVED WITH GARLIC CROSTINI & TOASTED SQUASH SEEDS
- PORCINI PECAN NORI ROLLS WITH GINGER PEAR PAPER & MISO TAHINI SAUCE
- RAW CORN CHIPS WITH AVOCADO PICO

PEPPER CRUSTED CASHEW CHEESE PLATE WITH JUNIPER TOFU & OLIVE TAPENADE

I serve this with Quick Pickled Beets (p. 199) and Quick Pickled Spicy String Beans (p. 200) along with Sesame Flax Crackers (p. 126), Hazelnut Rye Crisps (p. 123), or Salted Rye Sablés (p. 153).

• MAKES 6–8 SERVINGS.

PEPPER CRUSTED CASHEW CHEESE

1 cup (250 mL) Cashew Cheese (p. 192)
1 tbsp cracked multi-colored peppercorns
⅛ tsp red pepper flakes
⅛ tsp fresh thyme
¼ tsp salt

Cover a mini-cupcake pan with plastic wrap and spoon Cashew Cheese into cups to form a mold. Cover with more plastic wrap and refrigerate for 1–4 hours, until firm.

In a shallow bowl, combine spices. When ready to serve, remove cheese from cups and roll top and sides in spices.

Makes 6–8 cheese molds, depending on size of cupcake pan.

JUNIPER TOFU

2 cups (500 mL) water
2 tbsp juniper berries, crushed
1 tbsp smoked salt
¼ cup (60 mL) brown sugar
1 tsp whole peppercorns
1 tsp dried thyme, or 2 sprigs fresh
3 bay leaves
2 tbsp whole coriander
3 whole cloves
1 tsp balsamic vinegar
3 tbsp red wine

1 1-lb (450-g) pkg medium firm or smoked tofu, drained and cut into ½ in (1 cm) slices
grapeseed oil, for frying
1 tbsp juniper berries
1 tsp ground black pepper
1 tsp smoked salt

In a saucepan on medium-high heat, bring water, 2 tbsp juniper berries, spices and herbs, vinegar, and wine to a boil, and stir until salt and sugar dissolve. Remove from heat, gently add tofu, and submerge. Let marinate at room temperature for 2 hours, or overnight in the refrigerator. Remove tofu from marinade and strain.

In a frying pan on medium-high heat, add enough oil to cover bottom of pan. Heat oil, then add tofu and fry for 4 minutes on each side, until golden brown. Drain on paper towels.

With a mortar and pestle, crush 1 tbsp juniper berries, pepper, and salt. Garnish top of each tofu piece with ¼ tsp before serving.

OLIVE TAPENADE

¼ cup (60 mL) chopped green olives with pimentos
¼ cup (60 mL) pitted and chopped kalamata olives
3 pickled garlic cloves or 2 fresh garlic cloves
2 tsp orange juice
¼ cup (60 mL) chopped fresh parsley

In a bowl, combine all ingredients.
Makes ¾ cup (185 mL).

TO PLATE:

assorted pickles and crackers
    (see suggestions on previous page)
heirloom tomatoes

Place Cashew Cheese on each plate. Place about 1 tsp tapenade beside cheese. Arrange 2 slices of tofu on each plate. Serve with assorted crackers, pickles, and heirloom tomatoes.

BAKED EGGPLANT SAMOSAS WITH ASSORTED CHUTNEYS & COCONUT SOUR CREAM

Pair these samosas with Brown Rice Risotto with Kidney Beans (p. 95) for a filling meal.

• **MAKES 8–10 SERVINGS.**

¼ tsp cumin seeds
1 tbsp refined coconut oil
1 tsp Garam Masala (p. 210)
½ tsp ground coriander
½ tsp smoked paprika
½ tsp ground turmeric
¼ tsp red pepper flakes
1 large onion, chopped
1¼ tsp salt
4 garlic cloves, minced
2 tbsp minced fresh ginger
2 large tomatoes, chopped
1 lb (500 g) eggplant, chopped
2 tbsp water
¼ cup (60 mL) chopped fresh cilantro
1 batch Coconut Pastry (p. 155)

In a large pot on medium heat, toast cumin seeds for 1 minute, until fragrant. Add coconut oil. When oil has melted, add remainder of spices and cook for another minute, stirring constantly, being careful not to let it scorch. Add onions and salt, and sauté until onions are translucent. Add garlic, ginger, and tomatoes and sauté for another 3 minutes. Add eggplant and water, reduce heat, and simmer for 15–20 minutes, stirring occasion-ally, until eggplant is soft and tender. Stir in the cilantro and set aside.

Preheat oven to 425°F (220°C).

On a lightly floured surface, roll out half dough recipe to ⅛-in (3-mm) thickness with floured rolling pin. Use a 6-in (15-cm) bowl or cookie cutter to cut out circles. Slice each circle in half. Place a heaping tbsp of eggplant mixture onto center of each half circle. Working with straight edge of half circle, fold edges toward each other so that straight edges meet vertically in center. Pinch edges together, then pinch half circle together to form a T-seal. Repeat with remaining filling and dough. On an unoiled baking pan, bake samosas for 12–15 minutes, until golden brown.

Makes 20–25 small samosas.

TO PLATE:
Coconut Sour Cream (p. 195)
Assorted chutneys (any or all of, p. 196–97)

Place 1–3 samosas on a plate and spoon 1 tbsp each assorted chutneys around perimeter along with 1 tbsp Coconut Sour Cream.

CRISPY OYSTER MUSHROOM, SQUASH BLOSSOM & SWEET POTATO TEMPURA WITH GINGER MISO SAUCE & SESAME SWEET RICE

Of all the deep-fried foods, tempura really wins it, because of how light everything still tastes. The oyster mushrooms give an amazing meaty texture not usually found in tempura dishes.

• **MAKES 6 SERVINGS.**

GINGER MISO SAUCE

1 tbsp grated fresh ginger
1 tbsp shiro miso
1 tbsp brown rice syrup
2 tsp tahini
1 tbsp seasoned rice vinegar
½ tsp wasabi powder
1 tsp tamari
2 tsp sesame oil
3 tbsp water

In a blender or food processor, combine all ingredients until smooth.

SESAME SWEET RICE

2 cups (500 mL) cooked short grain white or brown rice
2 tbsp toasted sesame seeds
2 tbsp chopped green onions
1 tbsp seasoned rice vinegar
¼ tsp dulse flakes

In a bowl, combine all ingredients and set aside.

CRISPY OYSTER MUSHROOM, SQUASH BLOSSOM & SWEET POTATO TEMPURA

½ cup (125 mL) white rice flour
1 tbsp spelt flour
¼ cup (60 mL) cornstarch
1 tsp salt
⅛ tsp baking soda
⅛ tsp baking powder
⅓ cup (80 mL) cold water
2 tsp seasoned rice vinegar
1 tsp sesame oil
1 tsp grapeseed oil
2 tbsp tamari
6 oyster mushrooms, trimmed
6 squash blossoms
1 white or orange fleshed sweet potato, sliced into ¹⁄₁₆-in (1.5-mm) slices
grapeseed or canola oil, for deep-frying

In a bowl, combine flours, cornstarch, salt, baking soda, and baking powder. In a separate bowl, combine cold water, vinegar, and sesame and grapeseed oils. Gently whisk wet ingredients into dry ingredients. In a separate shallow bowl, add tamari.

In a deep fryer or pot on high, heat 3 in (8 cm) oil to 350°F (180°C). Dip oyster mushrooms into tamari, then coat with tempura batter and drop into hot oil. Fry for 1 minute, turn over, then fry for 1 more minute. Drain on paper towels. Dip squash blossoms and sweet potatoes in tempura batter and fry for about 2 minutes, until slightly golden. Drain on paper towels.

TO PLATE:

Using a circle mold, place ⅓ cup (80 mL) rice in the center of a shallow bowl. Place 1 tempura mushroom, 1 blossom, and a few slices of sweet potato on top of rice. Pour 2 tbsp Ginger Miso sauce into small bowls, 1 for each guest. Serve with chopsticks if desired.

Crispy Oyster Mushroom, Squash Blossom & Sweet Potato Tempura with Ginger Miso Sauce & Sesame Sweet Rice, 28–29

BRAZIL NUT SEA PÂTÉ WITH APPLES & SPRING ONIONS

I serve this pâté, reminiscent of tuna, on Sesame Flax Crackers (p. 126) or toasted on Crispy Flatbread Crackers (p. 121) with Coconut Melting Cheese (p. 194) on top.

• **MAKES 1¾ CUPS (415 ML).**

1 cup (250 mL) raw Brazil nuts, soaked in 2 cups
    water for at least 4 hours
½ cup (125 mL) raw sunflower seeds, soaked in 1 cup
    (125 mL) water for at least 4 hours
2 small garlic cloves
2½–3 tsp lemon juice, to taste
2½–3 tsp tamari, to taste
¼ tsp red pepper flakes
¼ tsp dulse flakes
¼ tsp kelp powder
3 spring onions, chopped, both green and white parts
½ cup (125 mL) cubed green apples
1 tbsp olive oil or 1 tbsp plus 1 tsp vegan mayonnaise

Drain soaked nuts and seeds and discard soaking liquid. In a food processor, purée garlic. Add nuts, seeds, lemon juice, tamari, red pepper flakes, dulse, and kelp. Pulse until well-blended but still coarse.

In a bowl, combine onions, apples, puréed mixture, and oil or vegan mayonnaise. With a spoon, stir until combined. Keep refrigerated.

APPLE SMOKED TOFU & CARAMELIZED ONION SPRING ROLLS WITH CARROT TAMARIND CHUTNEY & AVOCADO AIOLI

Smoky and sweet flavors are paired here with cool and creamy avocado and spicy carrots.

• **MAKES ABOUT 15 SPRING ROLLS.**

AVOCADO AIOLI

½ avocado
2 tbsp fresh cilantro
1 tsp lime juice
½ tsp Dijon mustard
1 tsp tahini
¼ tsp salt
¼ tsp ground black pepper
1 tbsp water
2 tbsp olive oil
½ jalapeño pepper, seeded and minced
1 garlic clove, minced
1 tbsp finely chopped fresh cilantro

In a blender or food processor, combine avocado, cilantro, lime juice, mustard, tahini, salt, black pepper, and water and blend until smooth. Slowly add oil and blend until emulsified. Stir in jalapeño, garlic, and chopped cilantro.

Makes ⅔ cup (160 mL).

APPLE SMOKED TOFU & CARAMELIZED ONION SPRING ROLLS

2 tsp refined coconut or grapeseed oil
1 cup thinly sliced onions, sliced lengthwise
1 tsp tamari

1 tsp balsamic vinegar
½ cup (125 mL) julienned smoked tofu
1 cup (250 mL) julienned Granny Smith apple
15 vegan spring roll wrappers
vegetable oil, enough to cover bottom of pot or deep fryer, at least 2½-in (6.5-cm) deep

In a frying pan on medium heat, melt oil. Add onions and cook for 3–5 minutes covered, stirring occasionally, until translucent. Add tamari and vinegar and continue to cook with the lid on, stirring occasionally, for 10 minutes, reducing heat if onions begin to burn. Remove from heat when onions are soft and caramelized.

In a bowl, mix onions, tofu, and apples. Place a spring roll wrapper on a wooden cutting board diagonally, so it forms a diamond shape. Place roughly 2 tbsp onion mixture on bottom corner of wrapper. Roll wrapper straight up and away from you to halfway point, then fold in sides and continue to roll. Dampen edges to seal. Set aside and cover with a damp tea towel. Repeat with remaining filling and wrappers.

In a deep fryer or pot, heat vegetable oil to 375°F (190°C). Add spring rolls, 2 or 3 at a time, being careful not to crowd pot. Fry for about 90 seconds, turn over, and fry for another 90 seconds, until golden. Drain on paper towels.

TO PLATE:

Carrot Tamarind Chutney (p. 196)

Cut each spring roll in half on a diagonal. Plate with 1 tbsp each aioli and chutney.

SEASONAL SQUASH & HEIRLOOM TOMATOES TOSSED WITH PEAR WALNUT BUTTER, SERVED WITH GARLIC CROSTINI & TOASTED SQUASH SEEDS

Pear Walnut Butter is amazing—great on popcorn, sautéed on pasta, or added as a finishing dollop to Butternut Squash & Apple Soup (p. 53).

• MAKES 6–8 SERVINGS.

SEASONAL SQUASH

1 small buttercup or butternut squash
½ tsp salt
2 tsp olive oil

Preheat oven to 375°F (190°C).

Cut squash in half lengthwise and seed. Reserve seeds for garnish. Rub each half of squash with salt and olive oil, then wrap in aluminum foil. Bake for 35 minutes, until squash is tender. Set aside until cool enough to handle.

TOASTED SQUASH SEEDS

squash seeds (pulp and fiber removed)
¼ tsp smoked paprika
¼ tsp salt

Preheat oven or toaster oven to 350°F (180°C).

In a small bowl, coat seeds with paprika and salt. Spread evenly on a small baking pan and bake for 5 minutes. Stir and turn seeds and bake for another 3–5 minutes, until they are dry and slightly golden. Set aside.

GARLIC CROSTINI

3 garlic cloves, minced or crushed
2 tbsp olive oil
1 tsp balsamic vinegar
12–14 slices day-old French or Sourdough Bread (p. 125)
½ tsp salt

Preheat oven to 425°F (220°C).

In a bowl, combine garlic, oil, and vinegar. Brush each side of bread with oil mixture and place on a baking sheet. Sprinkle with salt. Bake for 8 minutes, then turn over and bake for another 8 minutes.

PEAR WALNUT BUTTER

½ pear
½ bulb garlic
1 tbsp olive oil
¼ cup (60 mL) toasted walnuts
1 tbsp nutritional yeast
1 tbsp + 1 tsp lemon juice
1 tbsp chopped fresh sage
¼ tsp Dijon mustard
¼ tsp salt

¼ tsp ground black pepper
3 tbsp olive oil

Preheat oven to 375°F (190°C).

    Wrap pear half in aluminum foil. Slice top off garlic bulb to expose the cloves. Make a packet with aluminum foil for garlic and olive oil. Bake pear and garlic for 25 minutes, or until pear is cooked through and garlic is soft.

    Let pear cool, then core and peel it. Once garlic has cooled, squeeze cloves out of skins. In a blender or food processor, combine pear and garlic with remainder of ingredients except 3 tbsp oil and blend until smooth. Slowly add oil and blend until emulsified.

Makes 1 cup (250 mL).

TO FINISH AND PLATE:

¼ cup (60 mL) Pear Walnut Butter
4 heirloom tomatoes, sliced into wedges
coarse salt, for garnish

Peel skin from cooked squash and cut into cubes. On medium-high, heat a frying pan. Add Pear Walnut Butter, tomatoes, and squash and sauté for 3 minutes, until warmed. Divide among 6 plates. Place 2 crostini on each plate. Sprinkle with squash seeds and coarse salt.

Seasonal Squash & Heirloom Tomatoes Tossed with Pear Walnut Butter, Served with Garlic Crostini & Toasted Squash Seeds, 34–35

Porcini Pecan Nori Rolls with Ginger Pear Paper & Miso Tahini Sauce, 38–39

PORCINI PECAN NORI ROLLS WITH GINGER PEAR PAPER & MISO TAHINI SAUCE

This dish can be made without the Pear Paper if you don't have a dehydrator; instead, add julienned pears to the rolls. The Porcini pâté is also great on toasted Sourdough Bread (p. 125).

• **MAKES 6–8 SERVINGS.**

PORCINI PECAN PÂTÉ

½ cup (125 mL) dried porcini mushrooms soaked in
    1 cup (250 mL) hot water for 20 minutes
    (reserve soaking liquid)
1 tsp grapeseed oil
1 medium onion, chopped
2 garlic cloves, chopped
½ tsp Dijon mustard
2 tsp tamari
1 tsp lemon juice
1 tsp seasoned rice vinegar
1 tsp Sriracha (hot Thai chili sauce)
1 cup (250 mL) toasted pecans
2 tsp tahini

While mushrooms are soaking, in a frying pan, heat oil and sauté onions until translucent. Add garlic, mustard, tamari, lemon juice, vinegar, and Sriracha. Drain mushrooms and reserve liquid. Add mushrooms and ½ cup (125 mL) soaking liquid to pan and sauté for 3 minutes. Remove from heat.

In a food processor, blend pecans and tahini with cooked mixture to form a smooth pâté. Add extra soaking liquid if needed.

GINGER PEAR PAPER

6 ripe pears
2 tsp lemon juice
3 tbsp grated fresh ginger
2 tbsp toasted sesame seeds

Chop pears and remove cores. In a blender or food processor, blend pears with lemon juice and ginger. Stir in sesame seeds.

On Silpat (non-stick) dehydrator trays, spread layer of pear purée in a ¼-in (6-mm) thick rectangle, the size of a sheet of nori. Dehydrate at 115°F (46°C) for 40 minutes, or until pear "paper" is dry enough to peel off tray, but not brittle.

Makes 6–8 sheets of paper.

MISO TAHINI SAUCE

2 tbsp tahini
2 tbsp lemon juice
2 garlic cloves
1 tsp tamari
½ tsp Dijon mustard
½ tsp grated fresh ginger
¼ tsp cayenne pepper
¼ cup (60 mL) water
1 tbsp shiro miso
½ cup (125 mL) olive oil

In a food processor or blender, purée all ingredients until smooth.

TO ASSEMBLE AND PLATE:

1 cup (250 mL) julienned carrots
2 avocados, sliced
1 cup (250 mL) sunflower sprouts
6–8 sheets nori

On a cutting board or wood counter, roll out a sushi mat. (If you don't have one, you can do this without.) Lay a sheet of pear paper on the mat, then a sheet of nori. Spoon 3 tbsp pecan pâté in a rectangle on bottom quarter of nori. Arrange a few carrots, slices of avocado, julienned pears if omitting pear paper, and sprouts on top of pâté. Tightly roll up nori sheet, away from you, using bamboo mat as an aid. Repeat with each sheet. Cut each roll into 6 slices and arrange on a plate. Top with 1 tbsp of Miso Tahini Sauce.

RAW CORN CHIPS WITH AVOCADO PICO

Sweet corn flavor with a classic pico, a Mexican condiment made with finely chopped raw vegetables, including tomatoes, tomatillos, peppers, and avocado.

• **MAKES 2 CUPS (250 ML).**

RAW CORN CHIPS

2 cups (500 mL) raw corn, about 3 cobs
⅓ cup (80 mL) ground golden flax seeds
1 tbsp chopped shallots
1 garlic clove
1 tbsp lime juice
½ tsp salt

In a blender or food processor, blend all ingredients. Let sit for 4 hours.

On Silpat (non-stick) dehydrator trays, spread mixture ⅛-in (3-mm) thick. Sprinkle with extra salt, to taste, and dehydrate at 115°F (46°C) for 13 hours, until crispy and dry.

After about 6 hours, when mixture is still soft but dry enough to peel off tray, use sharp kitchen shears to cut into triangles. Continue to dehydrate for another 7 hours. Break apart and store in a sealed container.

Makes about 20 chips.

AVOCADO PICO

1 large avocado, cut into small cubes
1 cup (250 mL) tomato, diced
½ jalapeño pepper, seeded and diced
2 tsp shallots, finely diced
1 small garlic clove, finely diced
2½ tsp lime juice
2 tbsp finely chopped fresh cilantro
salt, to taste

In a bowl, combine all ingredients.

TO PLATE:

Serve pico in a small bowl with a bowl of your home-made chips beside it.

SOUPS & STOCKS

- CONDENSED SIMPLE STOCK
- MUSHROOM CONSOMMÉ
- SPICED PEANUT & YAM SOUP WITH PICKLED STRING BEANS & SWEET COCONUT BREAD
- SPLIT PEA BISQUE WITH MINTED COCONUT CREAM & CUMIN CROUTONS
- BLACK BEAN SOUP WITH COCONUT SOUR CREAM & PINE NUT PARMESAN
- CARAMELIZED ONION BISQUE WITH ROASTED GARLIC TOAST
- BUTTERNUT SQUASH & APPLE SOUP WITH CHIPOTLE APPLE REDUCTION, COCONUT SOUR CREAM & ROASTED SQUASH SEEDS
- FENNEL PORTOBELLO SOUP WITH SMOKE-INFUSED OLIVE OIL
- BEET & CABBAGE SOUP WITH COCONUT SOUR CREAM & ROSEMARY OIL
- SHIITAKE DASHI WITH SNOW PEAS & OYSTER MUSHROOM & TEMPEH WONTONS
- CARROT GINGER SOUP WITH LEMON BASIL CREAM
- WATERMELON RED PEPPER GAZPACHO

CONDENSED SIMPLE STOCK

I like to put a lot of my vegetable ends (from chopped onions, remains of roasted garlic bulbs, carrots, leeks, or celery) and mushroom and parsley stems into a large freezer bag—my "stock bag"—and store it in the freezer. Once the bag is full, I'm ready to make stock. This stock is reduced so it won't take up too much room; freeze it in ice-cube trays, then store in a freezer bag. When making soup from it, add water to the concentrated stock (¼ cup for each cube of stock).

• **MAKES ROUGHLY 6 CUPS (1.5 L) STOCK.**

1 1-gal (4-L) stock bag
2 tbsp olive oil
¼ cup (60 mL) dry white wine, or 2 tbsp white wine
    vinegar
2 sprigs fresh thyme
2 sprigs fresh rosemary
½ tsp coriander seeds
3 bay leaves
3 tsp salt
1 tbsp whole peppercorns
12 cups (3 L) water

Remove full stock bag from freezer. In a large soup pot on medium-high, heat olive oil, then add contents of the stock bag (no need to defrost). Sauté until vegetables soften, about 5–10 minutes. Add wine or vinegar and cook for another 5 minutes. Add herbs, salt, peppercorns, and water and bring to a boil.

Once it boils, reduce heat and simmer for 2 hours, until stock has reduced by half. Remove from heat. Let stock cool completely, even overnight if desired, before straining out vegetables, herbs, and peppercorns with a fine mesh strainer. If not using right away, freeze in ice cube trays, then store frozen cubes in a freezer bag.

MUSHROOM CONSOMMÉ

When I cook with mushrooms, I save the stalks in my "stock bag" (p. 45) in the freezer.
This is great as a clear soup or stock for risotto.

• **MAKES 8 CUPS (2 L).**

1 tbsp grapeseed oil
2 medium onions, roughly chopped
2 tsp salt
4 garlic cloves, smashed
4 cups (1 L) mushroom stalks (portobello, oyster,
    cremini, shiitake—any mix)
1 sprig fresh sage
1 sprig fresh rosemary
½ cup (125 mL) dry white wine
1 tsp tamari
1 tsp whole peppercorns
10 cups (2.5 L) water

In a large soup pot on medium-high, heat oil, then sauté onions and salt until onions are translucent. Add garlic, mushroom stalks, sage, and rosemary and cook for 3 minutes. Add wine, tamari, and peppercorns and cook for 5 minutes. Add water and bring to a boil. Once it boils, reduce heat and simmer, uncovered, for 30 minutes. Remove from heat.

When stock has cooled, strain and discard vegetables, herbs, and spices.

SPICED PEANUT & YAM SOUP WITH PICKLED STRING BEANS & SWEET COCONUT BREAD

Simple and filling, this spiced and creamy soup pairs perfectly with warm Sweet Coconut Bread, a favorite menu item at VSS.

• **MAKES 8–10 SERVINGS.**

SPICED PEANUT & YAM SOUP

2 tbsp coconut oil
1 tsp ground cumin
1 tsp ground cinnamon
1½ tsp ground coriander
½ tsp red pepper flakes
1 large onion, chopped
5 garlic cloves, smashed
2 tbsp grated or finely diced fresh ginger
4 cups (1 L) cubed and peeled yams
⅓ cup (80 mL) smooth natural peanut butter (I use Valencia, but any will work)
1 cup (250 mL) coconut milk
6 cups (1.5 L) stock (p. 45) or water
salt and ground black pepper, to taste
juice of 1 lime, to finish

In a large soup pot on medium-high heat, melt coconut oil. Add spices and red pepper flakes and cook until fragrant, just under 1 minute. Add onions and sauté until translucent. Add garlic and ginger and sauté for another 2 minutes. Add yams and continue cooking. Add a splash of stock if necessary to keep from scorching.

While yams cook, in a bowl, whisk peanut butter with coconut milk until smooth. Add to yams and follow with remainder of stock. Bring to a boil, then reduce heat, and simmer for 15 minutes, until yams are soft. Season with salt and pepper to taste.

In a blender or with an immersion blender, purée soup until smooth. Be careful when blending hot liquids. Add lime juice just before serving.

TO PLATE:

Sweet Coconut Bread (p. 126)
Quick Pickled Spicy String Beans (p. 200)

Ladle a serving of soup into a bowl. Add a garnish of coconut milk and a pickled string bean sliced in half lengthwise. Serve with a wedge of warm Sweet Coconut Bread.

SPLIT PEA BISQUE WITH MINTED COCONUT CREAM & CUMIN CROUTONS

Split peas, or dried field peas, require no soaking before cooking, which means it's relatively quick to prepare a filling soup like this one. Cumin and mint add an exotic layering of flavors to the hearty soup.

• MAKES 10–12 SERVINGS.

SPLIT PEA BISQUE

1 tbsp grapeseed oil
1 medium onion, chopped
1 roasted garlic bulb (p. 189), skins removed (reserve oil)
1 tsp smoked or regular salt
1 tsp ground black pepper
1 tsp fresh thyme
¼ cup (60 mL) dry white wine
2 cups green split peas, rinsed
6 cups (1.5 L) stock (p. 45)
1 bay leaf
2 tsp white wine vinegar

In a large soup pot on medium-high, heat oil, then sauté onions until translucent. Add roasted garlic cloves, salt, pepper, and thyme. Add wine and sauté for about 2 minutes, until wine has reduced. Add split peas, stock, bay leaf, and white wine vinegar. Bring to a boil, then reduce heat to a simmer. Cook for 20 minutes, or until peas are tender. Discard bay leaf.

In a blender or with an immersion blender, purée soup until smooth. Be careful when blending hot liquids.

MINTED COCONUT CREAM

¼ cup (60 mL) coconut milk
3 tbsp chopped fresh mint

In a blender, purée coconut milk and mint until smooth.

CUMIN CROUTONS

2 cups (500 mL) cubed day-old bread
2 tsp oil, a mix of roasted garlic oil and olive oil
1 tsp whole cumin seeds
½ tsp salt

Preheat oven to 425°F (220°C).
In a bowl, toss bread cubes with oil, cumin seeds, and salt. Spread on an unoiled cookie sheet and bake for 5 minutes, turn over and bake for another 5 minutes, until golden brown.

TO PLATE:

Ladle a serving of bisque into a bowl. Garnish with 1 tbsp of Minted Coconut Cream and a few croutons.

BLACK BEAN SOUP WITH COCONUT SOUR CREAM & PINE NUT PARMESAN

I recommend that you cook from dried beans, but if you don't have the time, you can use canned beans with added salt (rinse them well before using).

• **MAKES 6–8 SERVINGS.**

BLACK BEAN SOUP

¼ tsp cumin seeds
2 tsp grapeseed oil
1 large Spanish onion, chopped
1 tsp salt
½ tsp ancho chili powder
½ tsp ground chipotle pepper
1 cup (250 mL) peeled and chopped potato
1½ cups (375 mL) cooked black beans
4 cups (1 L) stock (p. 45) or water
1 tsp lime juice

In a large soup pot on medium-high heat, toast cumin seeds until fragrant. Add oil and onions and sauté until onions are translucent. Add salt, chili, and chipotle, and cook for another minute before adding potatoes and black beans. Add stock and bring to a boil. Reduce heat and simmer for 20 minutes. Add lime juice and, using an immersion blender or blender, purée soup until smooth. Be careful when blending hot liquids.

Makes 6 cups (1.5 L).

TO PLATE:

Coconut Sour Cream (p. 195)
Pine Nut Parmesan (p. 193)

Ladle soup into a shallow bowl. Sprinkle with 2 tsp of crumbled Pine Nut Parmesan and drizzle with 2 tsp of Coconut Sour Cream.

CARAMELIZED ONION BISQUE WITH ROASTED GARLIC TOAST

A deconstructed French onion soup, served with cheesy sourdough toast.

• **MAKES 6–8 SERVINGS.**

FRENCH ONION BISQUE

2 tbsp olive oil
2 large yellow onions, halved and sliced thinly,
    lengthwise
¾ tsp salt, to taste
2 tsp balsamic vinegar
¼ cup (60 mL) dry white wine
¼ tsp Dijon mustard
½ tsp tomato paste
½ tsp ground black pepper
¼ tsp red pepper flakes
¼ tsp fresh thyme
1 bay leaf
½ roasted garlic bulb (p. 189), skins removed
    and minced
5 cups (1.25 L) stock (p. 45)

In a large soup pot on medium-low, heat oil then sauté onions and salt for 10 minutes, stirring occasionally. Add vinegar and continue to cook for another 10 minutes until onions are soft and golden.

Increase heat to medium and add ⅓ of wine. Sauté for 2 minutes and repeat with another ⅓ of wine. Repeat until wine is gone.

Add mustard, tomato paste, pepper, red pepper flakes, thyme, and bay leaf. Add garlic and stir for 1–2 minutes. Add stock and bring to a boil. Reduce heat and simmer for 15 minutes.

Discard bay leaf. With an immersion blender or in a blender, purée half the soup until smooth (optional). Be careful when blending hot liquids. Return to pot and gently reheat.

ROASTED GARLIC TOAST

10 slices Sourdough (p. 125) or French bread
Coconut Melting Cheese (p. 194)

Preheat oven to 425°F (220°C).
On an unoiled baking sheet, place slices of bread. Spread generously with Coconut Melting Cheese and bake for 10 minutes, or until bread is golden brown and cheese is bubbly. If necessary, heat oven to broil to get the cheese bubbly, if you find the bread is toasting too quickly. Broil for 2–4 minutes, checking frequently to make sure it doesn't burn.

TO PLATE:

Serve in classic onion soup bowls topped with 1 or 2 slices of toast.

BUTTERNUT SQUASH & APPLE SOUP WITH CHIPOTLE APPLE REDUCTION, COCONUT SOUR CREAM & ROASTED SQUASH SEEDS

Even in squash season, I can never get my hands on enough squash. This soup is one of my classic VSS recipes, smooth and creamy with a hint of spice and sweetness.

• **MAKES 10–12 SERVINGS.**

BUTTERNUT SQUASH & APPLE SOUP

1 medium butternut squash
2 tbsp grapeseed oil
¼ tsp garam masala (p. 210)
1 tsp smoked paprika
½ tsp ground cinnamon
1 tbsp brown sugar (optional)
½ tsp each salt and pepper
1 whole garlic bulb
3 tbsp olive oil
1 medium onion, chopped
2 tsp salt
1 tbsp grapeseed oil
1 white-fleshed sweet potato, peeled and chopped
1 apple, peeled and chopped
1 tsp apple cider vinegar
½ tsp cayenne pepper
½ tsp ground black pepper
8 cups (2 L) water or stock (p. 45)

Preheat oven to 350°F (180°C).

With a large knife, remove stalk from squash. Cut squash in half lengthwise. With a spoon, scoop out seeds and set aside.

On a baking pan or dish with at least ½-in (1-cm) lip, place squash face up. Drizzle oil evenly on both halves.

Sprinkle garam masala, smoked paprika, cinnamon, brown sugar (if using), and salt and pepper on squash halves. Fill pan with enough water to cover bottom with about ¼–½ in (½–1 cm) water. Bake for 20 minutes. Carefully turn squash halves so they are resting face down in water, then bake for another 20 minutes, until soft. Set aside to cool a little.

Cut tops off garlic bulb to expose cloves. Place in aluminum foil and fold foil to form a small bowl. Pour in 3 tbsp olive oil and fold foil to create a sealed packet. Set in a small oven-proof bowl and bake with squash for 25 minutes, or until garlic is soft and fragrant. Set aside.

Meanwhile, in a large soup pot on medium-high, heat grapeseed oil, then sauté onions and salt until onions are translucent. Add sweet potato, apple, cider vinegar, cayenne, and black pepper and cook for another 3 minutes. Add the water or stock and bring to a boil. Reduce heat to a simmer.

When squash is cool enough to handle, remove skin with a knife and discard. Roughly chop squash. Add squash and water from pan to soup. Add roasted garlic and oil to soup. Simmer for about 10 minutes, until sweet potato is soft. In a blender or with an immersion blender, purée soup until smooth. Be careful when blending hot liquids.

ROASTED SQUASH SEEDS

squash seeds reserved from squash (fiber and pulp removed)
¼ tsp salt
¼ tsp smoked paprika

Preheat oven or toaster oven to 350°F (180°C).
In a small bowl, coat seeds with salt and paprika. Spread seeds evenly on a small baking pan and bake for 5 minutes. Stir and turn seeds and bake for another 3–5 minutes, until dry and slightly golden.

TO PLATE:

Chipotle Apple Reduction (p. 205)
Coconut Sour Cream (p. 195)

Ladle a serving of soup into a bowl. Drizzle with 1 tsp of Chipotle Apple Reduction and a spoonful of Coconut Sour Cream. Top with a few of the roasted squash seeds.

FENNEL PORTOBELLO SOUP WITH SMOKE-INFUSED OLIVE OIL

This savory soup has been known to seduce even the most stubborn mushroom skeptic.

• **MAKES 10–12 SERVINGS.**

FENNEL PORTOBELLO SOUP

1 roasted garlic bulb (p. 189), skins removed
2 tsp grapeseed oil
1 large onion, chopped
1 fennel bulb, chopped
1 tsp salt
8 portobello mushroom caps, chopped
1 tbsp fresh sage
1 tbsp fresh rosemary
½ tsp ground black pepper
¼ tsp red pepper flakes
2 tsp tamari
1 tsp white wine vinegar
½ cup (125 mL) champagne or dry white wine
8 cups (2 L) stock (p. 45) or water

While garlic is roasting, in a large soup pot on medium-high, heat oil, then sauté onions, fennel, and salt until onions are translucent. Add portobellos, sage, and rosemary and cook until soft. Add pepper, red pepper flakes, tamari, and vinegar. Add wine and cook for 2 minutes before adding stock or water. Bring to a boil, then reduce heat and simmer for 20 minutes. Add roasted garlic cloves.

In a blender or with an immersion blender, purée soup until smooth. Be careful when blending hot liquids.

TO PLATE:

Smoked-Infused Olive Oil (p. 206)
smoked salt, for garnish

Ladle a serving of soup into a bowl and drizzle with ½ tsp of Smoke-Infused Olive Oil. Finish with a little sprinkle of smoked salt.

BEET & CABBAGE SOUP
WITH COCONUT SOUR CREAM & ROSEMARY OIL

Not your grandmother's borscht. This soup pairs amazingly with Hazelnut Rye Crisps (p. 123).

• **MAKES 4–6 SERVINGS.**

BEET & CABBAGE SOUP

2 tsp grapeseed oil
1 medium onion, diced
4 garlic cloves, minced
¼ tsp whole coriander seeds, crushed
½ tsp fresh chopped rosemary
½ tsp ground black pepper
1 tsp salt
¼ tsp cayenne pepper
½ tsp tomato paste
2½ cups (625 mL) peeled and cubed beets
1½ cups (375 mL) red cabbage, shredded
2 tbsp red wine (or use red wine vinegar and omit
    apple cider vinegar)
1 tsp balsamic vinegar
1 bay leaf
5 cups (1.25 L) stock (p. 45)
1 tsp apple cider vinegar
salt, to taste (optional)

In a pot on medium, heat oil, then sauté onions until translucent. Add garlic, coriander, rosemary, pepper, salt, cayenne, and tomato paste. Add beets and cabbage, stirring constantly. Add wine and reduce for 2 minutes. Add balsamic vinegar. Add bay leaf and stock and bring to a boil. Reduce heat and simmer for 20 minutes, until beets are tender. Add cider vinegar and season with salt, if needed. Discard bay leaf.

In a food processor or blender, purée 1 cup of soup, then return to the pot (optional). Be careful when blending hot liquids.

TO PLATE:

Rosemary Olive Oil (p. 206)
Coconut Sour Cream (p. 195) or Cashew Cheese (p. 192)

Ladle a serving of soup into a bowl. Drizzle with ½ tsp Rosemary Oil and 1 tsp Sour Cream or Cashew Cheese.

SHIITAKE DASHI WITH SNOW PEAS & OYSTER MUSHROOM & TEMPEH WONTONS

Traditional dashi is a clear soup stock in Japanese cooking, usually made with bonito flakes (from tuna). This version uses dried shiitakes, which you can find in Asian markets, and kombu, a type of seaweed. Do not wash the kombu, as it comes with a white residue on it, which is a big part of its flavor. Dashi is also a great base for miso soup.

• **MAKES 8–10 SERVINGS.**

OYSTER MUSHROOM & TEMPEH WONTONS

8 oz (230 g) tempeh, cubed
1 recipe Ginger Miso Sauce (p. 28)
1 tsp grapeseed oil
¼ lb (125 g) oyster mushrooms, stalks removed and reserved for dashi, below
¼ tsp red pepper flakes
1½ tsp tamari
1 tbsp stock (p. 45) or water
1 tsp seasoned rice vinegar
2 tbsp chopped cilantro
3 tbsp chopped green onion
13-oz (370-g) pkg square or round vegan wonton wrappers

In a bowl, combine tempeh and Ginger Miso Sauce and marinate for 4 hours or overnight in refrigerator.

In a frying pan on medium-high, heat oil then add tempeh, reserving marinade. Fry for 5 minutes, then turn over to brown evenly. Add oyster mushrooms and continue cooking until soft. Reduce heat to medium and add red pepper flakes, tamari, stock, vinegar, and reserved marinade. Cook for another 5 minutes.

In a food processor, add tempeh mixture, cilantro, and green onions. Pulse until evenly ground.

On a clean work surface like a cutting board, lay out a few wonton wrappers. Keep a small bowl of water near you. Place 1 tsp of mushroom and tempeh filling in middle of each wrapper. With your finger or a small brush, dampen perimeter of wrapper. Fold in half, pressing edges closed and pushing out any air bubbles. Place on a parchment-lined cookie sheet and cover with damp tea towel or paper towel. Repeat until filling is used up.

At this point, you can freeze wontons on the cookie sheet, transferring to freezer bag or container once frozen, or you can use right away. They will keep, covered in refrigerator, for 1 day.

Makes 50 wontons.

Bring a large pot of salted water to boil on high heat. Drop in wontons and return to a boil. Boil for 3 minutes (5 minutes if frozen), until they float to the surface. Strain.

SHIITAKE DASHI

4 dried shiitake mushrooms
1 6-in (15-cm) piece dried kombu
½ cup (125 mL) oyster mushroom stalks (reserved
   from wontons)
6 cups (1.5 L) water
2 tbsp tamari
1 tbsp seasoned rice vinegar
1½ cups (375 mL) snow peas, trimmed

Soak shiitakes, kombu, and oyster mushroom stalks in water for 4 hours. Use a plate or inverted pot lid to keep mushrooms submerged. Discard kombu. In a soup pot on medium-high heat, bring water and mushrooms to a boil. Once boiling, remove shiitakes. Add tamari and rice vinegar and simmer for 3 minutes. Discard oyster mushrooms and add snow peas. Simmer for 2 minutes before serving.

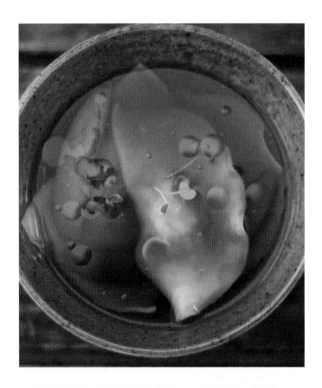

TO PLATE:

sesame oil, to finish
micro wasabi sprouts, about 1 tsp per serving, for garnish

Place 4 wontons in each bowl. Ladle a serving of dashi into each bowl along with 5 snow peas. Drizzle with ½ tsp sesame oil and top with wasabi sprouts.

ON MAKING MISO SOUP

Miso should not be boiled; at high temperatures, it loses nutritional value. To make miso soup, stir a small amount of hot water into a bowl with desired amount of miso paste, then add this to the soup at the end of the cooking process; slowly raise the temperature, but do not let the soup boil after adding miso.

CARROT GINGER SOUP WITH LEMON BASIL CREAM

A spicy soup with a hint of Thai flavor.

• **MAKES 10–12 SERVINGS.**

CARROT GINGER SOUP

1 tsp refined coconut or grapeseed oil
½ tsp whole coriander seeds
⅛ tsp fennel seeds
¼ tsp red pepper flakes
1 large onion, chopped
1¼–2 tsp salt, to taste
4 garlic cloves, crushed
1 tbsp grated or minced ginger
1 lemongrass stalk
5 cups (1.25 L) chopped carrots
1 cup (250 mL) peeled and chopped yams
1 bay leaf
8 cups (2 L) stock (p. 45)
2 tsp agave nectar
1 tsp lime juice
salt, to taste

In a soup pot on medium-high heat, melt coconut oil. Add coriander, fennel, and red pepper flakes and fry for 1 minute before adding onions and salt. Sauté until translucent. Add garlic, ginger, lemongrass, carrots, and yams and continue to sauté for 3 minutes. Add bay leaf and stock and bring to a boil. Reduce heat and simmer for 30 minutes. Add agave nectar and lime juice. Season with salt if needed.

Remove from heat and discard lemongrass stalks and bay leaf. In a blender, or with an immersion blender, purée soup until smooth. Be careful when blending hot liquids.

Makes 12 cups (3 L).

LEMON BASIL CREAM

¼ cup (60 mL) coconut milk or Coconut Sour Cream (p. 195)
¼ cup (60 mL) loosely packed fresh lemon basil (or regular) leaves

In a blender, blend coconut milk and basil. Strain with a fine mesh strainer.

TO PLATE:

Portion soup into shallow bowls and drizzle 1 tsp Basil Cream over soup.

WATERMELON RED PEPPER GAZPACHO

A surprising and colorfully refreshing chilled summer soup. It's great with yellow peppers and yellow watermelons, too!

• **MAKES 6–8 SERVINGS.**

1 red bell pepper, roughly chopped
2 tsp lime juice
½ red jalapeño, seeded and chopped
8 cups (2 L) cubed watermelon

In a blender, purée all ingredients. Chill thoroughly.

FOR GARNISH:
ground black pepper
about ½ cup (125 mL) micro basil sprouts
about ½ cup (125 mL) micro cilantro sprouts

TO PLATE:
Ladle a serving of soup into a bowl. Garnish with ground pepper and 1 tsp each fresh basil and cilantro sprouts.

SALADS

- SESAME AVOCADO QUINOA PILAF WITH FRIED SWEET PLANTAIN, CARAMELIZED RAMPS
  & MINTED COCONUT CREAM
- APPLE BEET SALAD WITH LEMON TAMARI VINAIGRETTE, BAKED HAZELNUT CHEESE
  & SESAME MUSTARD
- LIGHTLY BATTERED SMOKE-BLANCHED CAULIFLOWER WITH RED QUINOA TABOULI
  & TAHINI DRESSING
- WINTER GREENS WITH MISO SESAME SHIITAKES, RADISH, GOMASHIO
  & GRAINY MUSTARD EMULSION
- MUSTARD ROASTED NUGGET POTATOES WITH CRISPY FENNEL & SMOKY PORTOBELLOS
- WARM ROASTED BEETS WITH WILD ARUGULA, BALSAMIC MAPLE PECANS
  & ORANGE VINAIGRETTE
- PINE NUT CAESAR WITH LAVENDER BALSAMIC CROUTONS & CRISPY OYSTER MUSHROOMS

SESAME AVOCADO QUINOA PILAF WITH FRIED SWEET PLANTAIN, CARAMELIZED RAMPS & MINTED COCONUT CREAM

Ramps, also referred to as wild leeks, have a short growing season in early spring, and are mostly prevalent on the East Coast. A mix between onions and garlic in flavor, ramps are mild enough to eat raw, and you can use the leaves as well as the stem.

• MAKES 6–8 SERVINGS.

CARAMELIZED RAMPS

2 tsp coconut oil
1 small bunch fresh ramps, greens trimmed off and set aside, and sliced in half
salt, to taste

In a frying pan on medium heat, melt coconut oil. Add ramps cut-side down and sprinkle with salt. When ramps have turned slightly golden, stir and reduce heat. Cover and cook until translucent and caramelized. Set aside.

SESAME AVOCADO QUINOA PILAF

1 cup (250 mL) uncooked quinoa
2 cups (500 mL) water
½ tsp salt
greens from the ramps (above), chopped
1 avocado, cubed
¼ cup (60 mL) chopped cilantro

In a saucepan on medium-high heat, toast quinoa for about 1 minute, stirring constantly before adding water and salt. Bring to a boil and cook, stirring occasionally for 10 minutes, until water level is just beneath quinoa. Cover and reduce heat to low, and continue to cook for

10 minutes. Remove from heat. On an unoiled baking sheet, spread quinoa to let cool evenly.

In a large bowl, combine greens, avocado, and cilantro and add cooked quinoa. Add dressing (below) and stir until combined.

DRESSING FOR PILAF

½ cup Coconut Sour Cream (p. 195)
2 tsp sesame oil
3 tbsp olive oil
salt and pepper, to taste

In a bowl, whisk Coconut Sour Cream with sesame and olive oil. Season with salt and pepper. Set aside.

MINTED COCONUT CREAM

¼ cup (60 mL) coconut milk
3 tbsp chopped fresh mint

In a blender, purée coconut milk and mint until smooth. Set aside.

FRIED SWEET PLANTAIN

2 tbsp coconut oil
1 sweet plantain, sliced into ¼-in (6-mm) thick
rounds
juice of 1 lime
salt, to taste

In a flat-bottomed frying pan on medium-high heat, melt coconut oil. Add plantain and fry both sides until golden brown. Sprinkle each side with salt and squeeze lime juice over plantains just before removing from pan. Drain excess oil from plantains on paper towel if you wish.

TO PLATE:

1 lime, cut into 6-8 wedges, for garnish

Place ⅓ cup (80 mL) pilaf in center of a plate. Top with 3 slices plantain and a couple caramelized ramps. Dot plate with Minted Coconut Cream and garnish with lime wedge.

APPLE BEET SALAD
WITH LEMON TAMARI VINAIGRETTE, BAKED HAZELNUT CHEESE & SESAME MUSTARD

Beets and apples are one of my favorite combinations, especially when served raw as in this bright and colorful salad.

APPLE BEET SALAD WITH LEMON TAMARI VINAIGRETTE

1 garlic clove, finely diced or crushed
1 tsp finely diced shallot
1 tbsp lemon juice
2 tsp tamari
1 tsp maple syrup
2 tsp chopped fresh rosemary
1 tsp chopped fresh sage
½ tsp red pepper flakes (optional)
¼ cup (60 mL) olive oil
2 medium beets, grated or julienned
2 green apples, grated or julienned

In a food processor or blender, blend all ingredients except beets and apples, until emulsified.

In a bowl, toss apples and beets together with vinaigrette. Marinate for at least 30 minutes in refrigerator.

BAKED HAZELNUT CHEESE

1 cup (250 mL) hazelnuts, soaked in 1 tbsp miso and 2 cups (500 mL) water overnight (reserve liquid)
2 tbsp lemon juice
1 tbsp tahini
1 tbsp nutritional yeast
1 tsp salt
1 garlic clove

Preheat oven to 350°F (180°C).

Drain hazelnuts, reserving soaking liquid. In a food processor or blender, purée hazelnuts with remainder of ingredients. Add reserved soaking liquid if mix is too dry. Blend until it just comes together, like an extremely wet dough.

On a lightly oiled baking sheet, crumble or drop the cheese in small chunks and bake for 10 minutes, until firm to the touch and slightly golden.

Makes 1 cup.

SESAME MUSTARD

2 tbsp tahini
2 tbsp lemon juice
2 garlic cloves
2 tsp tamari
¼ tsp cayenne pepper
2 tsp Dijon mustard
2 tsp maple syrup
½ tsp grated fresh ginger (optional)
⅓ cup (80 mL) olive oil
2 tbsp water

In a food processor or blender, purée all ingredients until smooth.

Makes ½ cup.

TO PLATE:

about 3–4 cups mixed greens, enough for 5 people

Place a small amount of mixed greens on a plate. Top with about ⅓ cup (80 mL) apples and beets. Spoon Sesame Mustard around perimeter of plate and sprinkle Hazelnut Cheese over apples and beets.

LIGHTLY BATTERED SMOKE-BLANCHED CAULIFLOWER WITH RED QUINOA TABOULI & TAHINI DRESSING

The cauliflower in this dish is so delicately battered that it stays light. It has a gentle, smoky palate.

• MAKES 6 SERVINGS.

LIGHTLY BATTERED SMOKE-BLANCHED CAULIFLOWER

10 cherrywood or hickory chips
1 qt/L water
2 tsp salt
½ head of cauliflower, separated into florets
¼ cup (60 mL) rice flour
¼ cup (60 mL) corn flour
¾ cup (185 mL) milk (nut, rice, etc.)
1 tsp lemon juice
1 tsp salt
vegetable oil, enough to fill a pot 2-in (5-cm) deep

Using a lighter, carefully smolder the smoke chips slightly. Add them to a large pot with water and salt on high heat. Place cauliflower in a strainer that fits pot. Dip strainer into boiling water and cook for 4 minutes. Fill a large bowl with cold tap water and ice cubes (you may wish to do this in the kitchen sink) and submerge cauliflower to stop the cooking process. Strain and set aside.

In a bowl, whisk together rice and corn flour, milk, lemon juice, and salt. In a pot on medium or in a deep fryer set to 350°F (180°C), heat oil. Dip cauliflower into batter then fry for 90 seconds, turn, then fry for another 90 seconds, until golden. Drain on paper towels. Serve hot.

RED QUINOA TABOULI

1 cup (250 mL) red quinoa
2 cups (500 mL) water
½ tsp salt
⅓ cup (80 mL) chopped fresh mint
1 cup (250 mL) chopped fresh parsley
⅓ cup (80 mL) finely chopped shallots
1 cup (250 mL) halved cherry tomatoes
1 avocado, chopped
¼ cup (60 mL) lemon juice
¼ cup (60 mL) olive oil
1 tsp salt
1 tsp ground black pepper
¼ tsp red pepper flakes

In a saucepan on medium-high heat, toast quinoa for about 1 minute, stirring constantly before adding water and salt. Bring to a boil and cook, stirring occasionally, for 10 minutes, until water level is just beneath quinoa. Cover and reduce heat to low and continue to cook for 10 minutes. Remove from heat. On an unoiled baking sheet, spread quinoa to let cool evenly.

In a bowl, combine cooked, cooled quinoa, mint, parsley, shallots, cherry tomatoes, and avocado. Set aside.

In another bowl, whisk lemon juice, oil, salt, pepper, and red pepper flakes until emulsified. Add this to quinoa mixture to coat. Stir gently and set aside.

TAHINI DRESSING

1 tbsp tahini
1 tbsp lemon juice
½ roasted garlic bulb, skins removed (p. 189)
2 tsp tamari
½ tsp Dijon mustard
¼ tsp cayenne pepper
2 tbsp water
¼ cup (60 mL) olive oil

In a blender or food processor, combine all ingredients except oil and blend until smooth. Slowly add the oil and blend until emulsified.

Makes ½ cup (125 mL).

TO PLATE:

Using a 3-in (8-cm) round mold, spoon ⅓ cup (80 mL) tabouli into center of a plate. Slice cauliflower florets in half. Place 1–2 floret halves on top of quinoa. Drizzle 1 tbsp of tahini dressing around edges of plate.

SALADS

WINTER GREENS WITH MISO SESAME SHIITAKES, RADISH, GOMASHIO & GRAINY MUSTARD EMULSION

There are many greens that grow year-round, making fresh salad not just for warm weather. This salad pairs perfectly with Shiitake Dashi (p. 60).

• **MAKES 6 SERVINGS.**

Winter Greens
6 cups (1.5 L) washed and trimmed winter greens
 (frisée, romaine, butterhead)
½ bunch green onions, chopped
1 bunch radishes, trimmed and sliced

In a large bowl, toss greens with just enough Grainy Mustard Emulsion (below) to lightly coat. Add green onions and radishes.

GRAINY MUSTARD EMULSION
1 garlic clove, minced
2 tsp grainy mustard
1 tbsp lemon juice
1 tbsp seasoned rice vinegar
1 tsp white wine vinegar
½ tsp salt
½ tsp ground black pepper
1 tbsp water
¼ cup (60 mL) olive oil

In a bowl, whisk together all ingredients except oil. Slowly add oil while whisking to emulsify.

TO ASSEMBLE AND PLATE:
Miso Sesame Shiitake Mushrooms (p. 190)
Gomashio (p. 211)

Place 1 cup (250 mL) greens on a plate. Top with shiitakes and sprinkle with gomashio. Spoon 2 tsp Grainy Mustard Emulsion around perimeter of plate.

MUSTARD ROASTED NUGGET POTATOES WITH CRISPY FENNEL & SMOKY PORTOBELLOS

Fingerling potatoes also work nicely with this recipe, which can be served hot or at room temperature. Try to choose the smallest potatoes for roasting.

• **MAKES 6–8 SERVINGS.**

MUSTARD VINAIGRETTE

2 garlic cloves
2 tbsp Dijon mustard
½ tsp Barbados-style habañero hot sauce
2 tbsp lemon juice
1 tbsp brown sugar or agave nectar
¼ tsp tomato paste
1 tsp fresh thyme
½ tsp fresh tarragon
½ tsp salt
¾ cup (185 mL) olive oil

In a blender or food processor, purée all ingredients except oil. While blender is running, slowly add oil and blend until smooth.

ROASTED NUGGET POTATOES

2 lb (1 kg) nugget potatoes, washed and cut in half
⅓ cup (80 mL) Mustard Vinaigrette

Preheat oven to 400°F (200°C).

In a bowl, toss potatoes with vinaigrette. Place potatoes in a baking dish and bake for 12 minutes, turn them over, then bake for another 12–13 minutes, until tender. Remove from oven and let cool to room temperature.

CRISPY FENNEL

½ fennel bulb, trimmed and sliced thinly lengthwise by hand or with a mandolin
2 tbsp orange juice
¼ cup (60 mL) cornstarch
1 tsp salt
vegetable oil, enough to cover small pot or deep frying pan 1½-in (4-cm) deep

In a bowl, combine fennel and orange juice. In a shallow bowl, sift cornstarch and salt together.

Heat oil to 350°F (180°C). Place ⅓ cup (80 mL) fennel slices in cornstarch and drop into oil. Fry for 1 minutes, then turn pieces over and fry for another 1 minute, until golden. Drain on paper towel. Repeat with remaining fennel.

SMOKY PORTOBELLO MUSHROOMS

3 portobello mushroom caps, sliced

Follow instructions for the Smoky Balsamic Marinade on p.190 for marinating mushrooms. On a Silpat (non-stick) dehydrator tray, lay portobello slices and dehydrate at 115°F (46°C) degrees for 30 minutes. Alternatively, heat 2 tsp of grapeseed oil and fry slices 3 minutes on each side. Set aside.

TO ASSEMBLE AND PLATE:

3 tbsp Mustard Vinaigrette
2 tbsp chopped fresh chives
½ lemon
coarse or flaked salt, to taste

In a bowl, combine cooled potatoes, portobello mushrooms, Mustard Vinaigrette, and chives. Use a 3-in (8-cm) round mold to pile ½ cup (125 mL) of potatoes in center of plate (or pile by hand). Top with slices of crispy fennel. Squeeze lemon juice over fennel and sprinkle with salt. Drizzle remaining vinaigrette around perimeter of plate.

WARM ROASTED BEETS
WITH WILD ARUGULA, BALSAMIC MAPLE
PECANS & ORANGE VINAIGRETTE

I still can't believe that I hated beets as a kid. Now I can practically eat beets at every meal. Roasting beets brings out the best of their flavor, keeping all the nutrients tucked inside.

WARM ROASTED BEETS

3 medium red or candy-striped beets
2 tsp olive oil
½ tsp salt

Preheat oven to 375˚F (190˚C).

    Wash beets and trim off tops and bottoms. Rub with oil and salt and wrap in aluminum foil. Bake for 35 minutes or until soft. When beets have cooled enough to handle, skins should just rub right off. Cut into wedges and set aside.

ORANGE VINAIGRETTE

¼ cup (60 mL) orange juice
1 tsp Dijon mustard
½ tsp agave nectar
1 garlic clove
½ tsp fresh thyme
salt and ground black pepper, to taste
¼ cup (60 mL) olive oil

In a blender or food processor, combine all ingredients except oil and blend until smooth. Slowly add oil and blend until emulsified.

Makes ½ cup (125 mL).

TO ASSEMBLE AND PLATE:

6 cups (1.5 L) washed wild arugula
¼ cup (60 mL) Orange Vinaigrette
Balsamic Maple Pecans (p. 200)

In a large bowl, combine Warm Roasted Beets, arugula, and Orange Vinaigrette.

    Place salad in middle of a serving bowl and top with Balsamic Maple Pecans.

PINE NUT CAESAR
WITH LAVENDER BALSAMIC CROUTONS
& CRISPY OYSTER MUSHROOMS

A rich, flavorful take on the very un-vegan-friendly original.

• **MAKES 8–10 SERVINGS.**

PINE NUT CAESAR DRESSING

¼ cup (60 mL) pine nuts
½ roasted garlic bulb (p. 189), skins removed
3 tbsp unsweetened almond or soy milk
2 tbsp lemon juice
1 tbsp white wine vinegar
1 tsp Dijon mustard
1 tsp brown rice syrup
2 tsp tamari
1 tbsp nutritional yeast
3 tsp capers
½ tsp ground black pepper
⅓ cup (80 mL) olive oil

Preheat oven or toaster oven to 350°F (180°C).

Toast pine nuts for 5 minutes, stirring halfway, until golden and fragrant. Let cool. In a blender or food processor, combine all ingredients except oil and blend until smooth. Slowly add oil and blend until emulsified.

Makes ¾ cup (185 mL).

LAVENDER CROUTONS

1 tsp dried lavender flowers, crushed
1 tbsp olive oil
2 tsp white wine vinegar
2¼ cups (530 mL) cubed day-old bread
   (about ½ a small loaf)
⅛ tsp salt
⅛ tsp ground black pepper

Preheat oven to 425°F (220°C).

In a large bowl, whisk lavender, oil, and vinegar. Add cubed bread and toss to coat. Spread on an unoiled cookie sheet and sprinkle with salt and pepper. Bake for 5 minutes, turn cubes over and bake for another 5 minutes, until golden brown.

Makes 2¼ cups (530 mL).

CRISPY OYSTER MUSHROOMS

1 cup (250 mL) trimmed and chopped oyster mushrooms
¼ cup (60 mL) cornstarch, sifted
1 tsp salt
grapeseed oil, enough to cover bottom of small frying pan ½-in (1-cm) deep
½ lemon

In a shallow bowl, generously coat mushrooms with sifted cornstarch and salt. In a frying pan on medium-high, heat oil to 325°F (160°C). Drop mushrooms into oil and fry each side, turning after 30 seconds. Drain on paper towels. Sprinkle with a little lemon juice and serve immediately.

TO ASSEMBLE AND PLATE:

I head romaine lettuce, washed and chopped
2 cups (500 mL) finely chopped mustard greens
2 cups (500 mL) finely chopped rainbow chard
3 tbsp capers
1 tsp flaked smoked salt
Pine Nut Parmesan (p. 193)

In a large bowl, toss lettuce, mustard greens, and chard with enough Pine Nut Dressing to coat. Add capers, and 1 cup (250 mL) croutons. In shallow bowls, portion salad and top with a few crispy oyster mushrooms. Sprinkle mushrooms with a pinch of smoked salt and Pine Nut Parmesan.

MAINS

- LENTIL WALNUT TOURTIÈRE WITH CARROT TAMARIND CHUTNEY & BALSAMIC REDUCTION
- BUTTERNUT SQUASH & ALMOND GNOCCHI SAUTÉED WITH SAGE GARLIC BUTTER
- YAM & WALNUT CROQUETTES WITH COCONUT SOUR CREAM, ANCHO BALSAMIC BEET REDUCTION & WILTED PEA SHOOTS
- BLUE CORN EMPANADAS WITH PECANS, BLACK BEANS, MOLE PIPIÁN, RED CABBAGE & AVOCADO
- BROWN RICE RISOTTO WITH KIDNEY BEANS & ANISE-TOASTED SUNFLOWER SEEDS
- PAN-FRIED PURPLE POTATO & CABBAGE DUMPLINGS WITH CILANTRO PESTO
- HAZELNUT-CRUSTED PORTOBELLOS WITH CARAMELIZED FENNEL PARSNIP MASH, RADICCHIO MARMALADE & BALSAMIC PORT REDUCTION
- LEEK & OYSTER MUSHROOM RISOTTO CAKES WITH YELLOW BEET REDUCTION
- PIPIÁN PESTO TORTELLINI WITH SEARED ASPARAGUS & ROASTED TOMATILLO SAUCE
- COCONUT FETTUCINE ALFREDO WITH SEARED BRUSSELS SPROUTS & CHERRY TOMATOES
- ROASTED GOLDEN BEET & WILD ARUGULA PESTO PIZZA WITH SESAME SHIITAKES & CASHEW CHEESE ON A QUINOA CAULIFLOWER CRUST
- WILD RICE DUMPLINGS WITH PUMPKIN LEMONGRASS CURRY
- MISO & JAPANESE EGGPLANT PIEROGIES WITH RAINBOW CARROT SHISO SLAW & COCONUT SOUR CREAM
- SHERRY-ROASTED ROOT VEGETABLES ON BROWN RICE KALE PILAF WITH TAHINI BUTTER

LENTIL WALNUT TOURTIÈRE WITH CARROT TAMARIND CHUTNEY & BALSAMIC REDUCTION

This is a very loose take on the traditional Quebecois meat pie eaten in the winter. I have never tasted one, but I love pies, so I came up with this savory vegan version.

• **MAKES 8 SERVINGS.**

LENTIL WALNUT TOURTIÈRE

2 tbsp grapeseed oil
1 medium onion, diced
¾ tsp salt
1 medium carrot, diced
½ tsp fresh thyme
¼ tsp smoked paprika
⅛ tsp cumin
½ tsp ground black pepper
¼ tsp red pepper flakes
8 cremini mushrooms, diced
⅓ cup (80 mL) dry white wine, or 1 tbsp plus
    1 tsp white wine vinegar
2 tsp tamari
1 tsp light miso
½ tsp Dijon mustard
2 ½ cups (625 mL) cooked green lentils
½ bulb roasted garlic (p. 189), minced, skins
    removed, or 4 garlic cloves, minced
⅓ cup (80 mL) stock (p. 45)

2 tbsp nutritional yeast
1 batch Shortcrust Pastry (p. 155)
½ cup (125 mL) finely chopped toasted walnuts
1 tsp milk (nut, rice, etc.)
2 tsp olive oil
2 tsp nutritional yeast
½ tsp tamari

Preheat oven to 400°F (200°C).

In a large pot on medium-high, heat oil. Add onions and salt and cook covered for 5 minutes; give it a stir half-way through cooking time. Add carrots, herbs and spices, and mushrooms. Continue cooking, stirring frequently. Add wine, 2 tsp tamari, miso, and mustard and cook down for 3 minutes. Add lentils, roasted garlic (if using), stock, and nutritional yeast and cook for 3 minutes while stirring. Remove from heat and set aside.

Roll out ½ of pastry into a 12-in (30-cm) circle, ¼-in (6-mm) thick. Fold gently in half and place onto 1 side of an 8-in (20-cm) pie dish. Unfold to cover entire dish and trim edges with a knife. Roll out other half of dough to same size and set aside.

Stir walnuts into lentils. Pour lentil mix into pie dish. Top with remaining crust. Trim edges with a knife and, using a fork or 2 fingers side by side, pinch edges of crust to seal. Poke a few holes on top of crust.

In a small bowl, whisk together milk, oil, yeast, and 1 tsp tamari. With a pastry brush, lightly brush this mixture over top of pie. Bake for 15 minutes. Reduce oven temperature to 350°F (180C) and bake for another 20 minutes, or until edges are golden brown.

TO PLATE:

Carrot Tamarind Chutney (p. 196)
Balsamic Reduction (p. 205)

Cut pie into 8 wedges. Serve 1 wedge per plate with 2 tbsp chutney. Drizzle 1 tsp Balsamic Reduction around plate.

BUTTERNUT SQUASH & ALMOND GNOCCHI SAUTÉED WITH SAGE GARLIC BUTTER

This light autumn meal takes time to prepare, but it is well worth it, given its amazing flavors. The gnocchi can also be frozen for future use.

• MAKES 4 SERVINGS AS A MAIN,
OR 6 AS A STARTER.

BUTTERNUT SQUASH & ALMOND GNOCCHI

**1 cup (250 mL) + 1 tbsp peeled and cubed butternut
   squash (about ¼ small squash)**
**1½ cups (375 mL) peeled and cubed russet potato
   (about 1 large potato)**
¼ cup (60 mL) almond butter
½ tsp salt
¼ tsp ground black pepper
⅛ tsp ground nutmeg
¼ tsp ground cinnamon
2 tsp olive oil
**1 cup (250 mL) spelt flour + additional ¾ cup
   (185 mL) for kneading and dusting**

In a pot with at least 1-in (2.5-cm) water, fill a steamer basket, bamboo steamer, or metal sieve with squash and potatoes. Cover and bring water to a boil on medium heat. Steam for 10 minutes, until squash and potatoes are very tender. Transfer to a bowl to let cool slightly.

If you have a ricer, rice the squash and potatoes, or use a potato masher and then use a fork to mash squash and potatoes thoroughly. Add almond butter, salt, pepper, nutmeg, cinnamon, and oil, and mash until combined. Slowly add 1 cup flour, ¼ cup (60 mL) at a time, until entire cup is used and a sticky dough forms.

Turn out onto a floured surface and gently knead until

smooth, for about 3 minutes, adding another ⅓ cup (80 mL) flour if needed. Generously flour a clean work surface. Gently roll out ⅓ cup (80 mL) dough at a time to form a ½-in (1-cm) thick cylinder. Use a sharp knife to cut cylinder into ½-in rounds. Place in a floured baking pan and cover with a tea towel. Repeat with remaining dough. (At this point, you can freeze dough to use at a later date, transferring to a freezer bag or container once frozen.)

Lightly oil a large glass baking dish and set aside. Bring a large pot of salted water with 1 tsp olive oil to a boil. Drop in gnocchi, about 10 at a time, and cook for 4 minutes. Gnocchi should rise to top of water. Using a sieve or slotted spoon, lift gnocchi out of water, place in glass baking dish, and cover. When all gnocchi are cooked, let rest in a single layer in baking dish for 1 hour before sautéing, or store, covered, overnight in refrigerator.

Makes about 75 gnocchi.

SAGE GARLIC BUTTER
1 roasted garlic bulb (p. 189), skins removed
2¼ tsp lemon juice
2 tbsp nutritional yeast

1 tbsp fresh sage leaves
2 tbsp olive oil
1 tsp white wine vinegar
¼ tsp salt
¼ tsp ground black pepper
¼ tsp red pepper flakes

In a blender or food processor, purée all ingredients until smooth. Set aside.

In a frying pan on medium heat, add 1 tbsp Sage Garlic Butter for every 18 gnocchi and sauté for 2 minutes, until gnocchi are slightly browned on both sides.

TO PLATE:
about 1 tbsp fresh sage leaves, for garnish

Place 10–15 gnocchi on a plate and garnish with ¼ tsp of fresh chopped sage.

YAM & WALNUT CROQUETTES WITH COCONUT SOUR CREAM, ANCHO BALSAMIC BEET REDUCTION & WILTED PEA SHOOTS

These croquettes are one of my favorite dishes. I have also used the filling to make dumplings served with Cashew Cheese (p. 192) and a dusting of ground chipotle peppers.

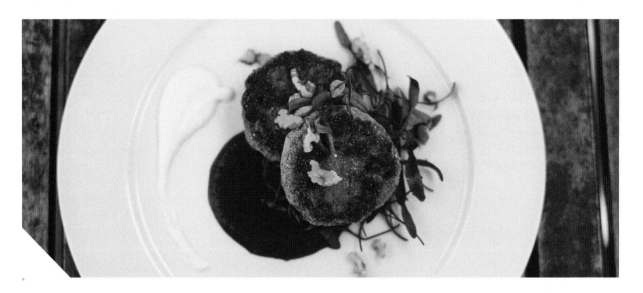

• **MAKES 6–8 SERVINGS.**

ANCHO BALSAMIC BEET REDUCTION

1 tbsp grapeseed oil
1 medium onion, chopped
1 tsp ancho chili powder
1 tbsp whole coriander seeds
2 whole cloves
½ tsp whole peppercorns
1 sprig fresh rosemary (about a finger long)
3 garlic cloves, smashed

2 tsp tamari
2 medium beets, peeled and chopped
¼ cup balsamic vinegar
2 cups (500 mL) stock (p. 45) or water (enough to just cover the tops of the beets in saucepan)

In a large saucepan on medium-high, heat oil. Add chopped onions, spices, and rosemary and cook until onions are translucent. Add garlic and tamari and cook for another 2 minutes. Add beets, vinegar, and stock. Bring to a boil, then reduce heat to medium-low. Simmer until ⅓ of liquid has reduced and beets are cooked, about 20 minutes.

Remove rosemary sprig, peppercorns, and cloves. In a blender, purée beet mixture, adding more water if necessary, until smooth. Be careful when blending hot liquids. This sauce can be made ahead of time and reheated.

YAM & WALNUT CROQUETTES

1 large yam
1 tbsp grapeseed oil
1 medium onion, chopped
½ tsp salt
½ tsp ground cinnamon
¼ tsp garam masala
¼ tsp cayenne pepper
1 tsp balsamic vinegar
1 cup (250 mL) toasted and roughly chopped walnuts
½ cup (125 mL) Cashew Cheese (p. 192)
¼ cup (60 mL) nutritional yeast
1 tsp salt
1 tsp ground black pepper
½ cup (125 mL) chickpea flour
½ tsp smoked paprika
½ tsp salt
grapeseed or walnut oil, for frying

Preheat oven to 375°F (180°C).

Wrap yam in aluminum foil and bake for 30–40 minutes. When soft, remove from oven and let cool. Peel off skin.

In a frying pan on medium, heat grapeseed oil. Stir in onions, sprinkle with salt, and cover pan. Cook for about 2 minutes, stir again, then continue to cook for another 2–3 minutes. Uncover and add spices and balsamic vinegar. Reduce heat to medium and cook down until onions are soft and caramelized.

In a large bowl add cooled, peeled yam. With a potato masher or immersion blender, mash until just smooth: should make about 1½ cups (375 mL). Stir in walnuts, Cashew Cheese, yeast, salt and pepper, and cooked onions. Use ⅓ cup (80 mL) of mix at a time to form croquettes ½-in (1-cm) thick. Set aside.

In a shallow bowl, combine chickpea flour, paprika, and salt. In a frying pan on medium-high heat, add generous coating of oil. Dredge croquettes in flour mix and fry each side for 2–3 minutes, until golden brown and crispy. Serve immediately or transfer to oven to keep warm.

WILTED PEA SHOOTS

1 tsp grapeseed oil
3 cups (750 mL) pea shoots, trimmed and washed
salt, to taste

In a frying pan on medium-high, heat oil. Add pea shoots and sauté, stirring constantly for 1–2 minutes, just until slightly wilted. Season with a little sprinkle of salt.

TO PLATE:

Coconut Sour Cream (p. 195)
¼ cup (60 mL) chopped fresh cilantro, for garnish
3 tbsp toasted chopped walnuts

Spoon about 1–2 tbsp beet reduction across middle of a plate. Place small pile of pea shoots in center and angle 2 croquettes on top. Place 1 tbsp Coconut Sour Cream on side of plate and garnish with chopped walnuts and fresh cilantro.

BLUE CORN EMPANADAS WITH PECANS, BLACK BEANS, MOLE PIPIÁN, RED CABBAGE & AVOCADO

Mole Pipián is a Mexican sauce that uses pumpkin or squash seeds instead of chocolate, which give it a beautiful green color. Avocado leaves are sold in Mexican food stores. If you can't find them, substitute 1 bay leaf and ¼ tsp crushed anise seeds.

• MAKES 8 SERVINGS.

MOLE PIPIÁN
6 tomatillos
1 jalapeño pepper
1 green bell pepper
2 tsp whole cumin seeds
2 tbsp grapeseed oil
1 medium Spanish onion, chopped
2 garlic cloves, smashed
2 dried avocado leaves
1½ cups (375 mL) pumpkin seeds
⅔–1 cup (160–250 mL) stock (p. 45)
1 tsp salt, to taste

Preheat oven to 325°F (160°C).

On an unoiled cookie sheet, roast whole tomatillos with jalapeño and bell peppers, for 20 minutes. When soft, remove from oven and let cool.

Meanwhile, in a dry frying pan on medium heat, toast cumin seeds until fragrant, then add oil. Add onions and garlic and sauté for 5 minutes, until onions are translucent.

Remove seeds from bell pepper and stalks from jalapeño and tomatillos. In a food processor or blender, purée roasted vegetables with onion mixture, garlic, avocado leaves, pumpkin seeds, and stock (if mixture is too thick, add more stock). Season with salt, to taste. This can be made ahead and reheated before serving.

RED CABBAGE
1 cup (250 mL) finely shredded red cabbage
2 tsp vinegar
½ tsp agave nectar
¼–½ tsp salt

In a bowl, combine all ingredients and let sit for 15 minutes before serving.

BLACK BEAN FILLING
¼ tsp cumin seeds
1 tsp grapeseed oil
1 medium Spanish onion, finely chopped
½ jalapeño pepper, finely chopped and seeded
3 garlic cloves, finely chopped
½ tsp salt
3 tbsp orange juice
1½ cups (375 mL) cooked black beans
¼ cup (60 mL) stock
1 tsp lime juice
salt, to taste

In a saucepan or large frying pan on medium-high heat, toast cumin seeds until fragrant. Add oil and onions and sauté until translucent. Add jalapeño pepper, garlic, and

salt. Stir in orange juice and simmer for 2 minutes. Stir in black beans and stock. Reduce heat and simmer for 3 minutes, stirring often. Add lime juice and season with extra salt if needed.

BLUE CORN EMPANADA DOUGH

½ cup (125 mL) fine blue cornmeal (or yellow if blue unavailable)
1 cup (250 mL) fine spelt or wheat flour
½ tsp salt
2 tbsp finely chopped toasted pecans
2 tbsp grapeseed or olive oil
¼ cup (60 mL) water

Preheat oven to 400°F (200°C).

In a bowl combine cornmeal, flour, salt, and pecans. Make a well in the center of dry mix and pour in oil and water. Mix until the dough starts to come together; add more water as needed. Try not to over-mix. Let dough rest, covered, for 20 minutes.

On a lightly floured surface, roll out about 2 tbsp dough to a 5-in (12-cm) wide circle, ⅛-in (3-mm) thick. Place ¼ cup (60 mL) black bean filling in middle of cir-

cle. Keep a small bowl of water nearby. Using your fingers or a pastry brush, wet edges then fold dough in half and, using a fork, press edges down to seal. Set on a baking pan dusted with cornmeal. Repeat with remaining bean filling and dough.

Bake empanadas for 12–15 minutes, until edges are golden brown.

Makes 8 empanadas.

TO PLATE:
1 avocado, cut into 8 slices
2–3 tbsp chopped fresh cilantro, for garnish

Spoon about 3 tbsp Mole Pipián onto a plate. Add 2 tbsp cabbage. Cut an empanada in half and place over mole, overlapping each half. Add a few slices of avocado and garnish with fresh cilantro.

BROWN RICE RISOTTO WITH KIDNEY BEANS & ANISE-TOASTED SUNFLOWER SEEDS

A simple and filling dish that's great when served with a simple green salad.

• MAKES 4–6 SERVINGS.

BROWN RICE RISOTTO WITH KIDNEY BEANS

¼ tsp whole cumin seeds
2 tbsp grapeseed oil
3 garlic cloves, minced
1 medium onion, chopped
½ tsp salt
¼ tsp ground black pepper
¼ tsp garam masala (p. 210)
¼ tsp ground turmeric
½ tsp chili powder
¼ tsp smoked paprika
¼ tsp red pepper flakes
1 tsp tomato paste
1 cup uncooked short grain brown rice
2 tbsp dry white wine
1 medium tomato, diced
1 cup (250 mL) peeled and cubed white
   sweet potatoes
1 cup (250 mL) cooked kidney beans
2½ cups (625 mL) stock (p. 45) or water

In a large pot in medium-high heat, toast cumin seeds for 1–2 minutes until fragrant. Add oil, garlic, and onions and sauté for 3 minutes, until onions are translucent. Add remainder of spices, tomato paste, and rice and stir constantly for about 3 minutes. When rice begins to look translucent, add wine and cook for another 1–2 minutes. Add tomatoes, sweet potatoes, and kidney beans and stir to combine.

Slowly add 1 cup of stock or water, stirring occasionally for 5 minutes; slowly stir in 1 more cup. Reduce heat and let simmer for 20 minutes, stirring occasionally to prevent scorching. When risotto starts to look thicker and water is absorbed, add another ½ cup (125 mL) stock or water, reduce heat to low, cover, and cook for 15 minutes, until rice is tender. Remove from heat and let sit for 5 minutes before serving.

TO PLATE:

coarse smoked salt, to taste
olive oil, to garnish
Anise-Toasted Sunflower Seeds (p. 201)

Portion risotto into shallow bowls. Sprinkle with smoked salt and a drizzle of olive oil, and top with the Anise-Toasted Sunflower Seeds.

PAN-FRIED PURPLE POTATO & CABBAGE DUMPLINGS WITH CILANTRO PESTO

These simple little dumplings pack a colorful and tasty surprise.

• MAKES 8 SERVINGS.

CILANTRO PESTO

2 tbsp Cashew Cheese (p. 192) or 3 tbsp roasted
    and chopped walnuts
1 garlic clove
½ fresh jalapeño pepper, seeded and chopped
3 tsp lime juice
½ tsp salt
2 cups (500 mL) lightly packed fresh cilantro
⅓ cup (80 mL) lightly packed basil leaves
¼ cup (60 mL) olive oil

In a blender or food processor, purée all ingredients until smooth.

Makes ¾ cup (185 mL).

PAN-FRIED PURPLE POTATO & CABBAGE DUMPLINGS

½ lb (250 g) purple potatoes, peeled, if necessary,
    and cubed, about 3½ cups (830 mL)
2 tbsp water
1 tbsp olive oil
½ roasted garlic bulb (p. 189), skins removed, minced
1 tbsp grapeseed oil
1 medium red onion, diced
1½ cups (375 mL) finely shredded red cabbage
½ tsp salt
¼ tsp ground black pepper
¼ tsp red pepper flakes
1 tsp tamari
2 tsp balsamic vinegar
13-oz (370-g) pkg round vegan wonton wrappers

In a pot filled with at least 1 in (2.5 cm) water on medium-high heat, place a 6-in (15-cm) diameter steam basket, add potatoes, cover, and bring to a boil. Steam for 15–20 minutes, until cooked through. Transfer potatoes to a bowl. Add 2 tbsp water, olive oil, and garlic and mash with a potato masher until smooth. Set aside.

In a frying pan over medium, heat grapeseed oil. Add onions and sauté until translucent. Add cabbage, salt, pepper, and red pepper flakes. Sauté for 2 minutes, then add tamari and vinegar. Reduce heat and continue to cook until cabbage and onions are soft. Add to potatoes and mix to combine well.

On a clean work surface like a cutting board, lay out a few wonton wrappers. Keep a small bowl of water nearby. Place 2 tsp Purple Potato filling in middle of each wrapper. With your finger or a small brush, dampen edges of each wrapper with water. Fold in half, pressing edges closed to seal. Position dumplings so seams face up; press slightly to create flat bottoms. Place on a parchment

lined cookie sheet and cover with damp tea towel or paper towel. Repeat with remaining filling and wrappers. (At this point, you can freeze the dumplings, transferring to a freezer bag or container once frozen. They will also keep covered in the refrigerator for 1 day.)

Makes 38–40 dumplings.

To pan-fry fresh dumplings: In a frying pan on medium, heat 1 tbsp grapeseed oil. Add dumplings, flat side down, and cover pan. Cook for 1–2 minutes, until bottoms are golden, then lay them on 1 side. Cook uncovered for 1 minute, then turn over and cook other side for 1 minute, until golden.

To pan-fry frozen dumplings: Remove from freezer 5–10 minutes before cooking. Let bottom side cook, covered, for 3 minutes, until golden, then cook each side, covered, for 1–2 minutes. Reduce heat if they start to brown too quickly.

TO PLATE:

¼ cup (60 mL) chopped fresh cilantro

On a square or rectangular plate, diagonally spread 1 tbsp Cilantro Pesto across middle. Place 5 dumplings across pesto. Garnish with 1 tsp cilantro.

HAZELNUT-CRUSTED PORTOBELLOS WITH CARAMELIZED FENNEL PARSNIP MASH, RADICCHIO MARMALADE & BALSAMIC PORT REDUCTION

This is a great winter dish, perfect for the holidays. The marmalade is a version of a French recipe passed down to a friend of mine and is surprisingly sweet and flavorful—an unusual use of such a bitter lettuce. (See recipe photo, p.82)

• MAKES 6 SERVINGS.

RADICCHIO MARMALADE

¼ cup (60 mL) olive oil or Earth Balance vegan
    margarine
1 head radicchio lettuce, finely chopped
½ cup (125 mL) maple syrup
¼ cup (60 mL) balsamic vinegar
½ cup (125 mL) orange juice
1 bay leaf
½ tsp fresh thyme
½ tsp ground black pepper
1 whole clove
½ cinnamon stick, about 1-in (2.5-cm) long
2 juniper berries, crushed

In a medium pot on medium heat, melt olive oil or vegan margarine. Add radicchio and sauté for 3 minutes. When radicchio begins to soften, add maple syrup and continue to cook for 5 minutes, until soft and caramelized. Add remainder of ingredients and bring to a boil. Reduce to a simmer and cook, stirring often, for about 10 minutes, until marmalade is thick and jam-like.

BALSAMIC PORT REDUCTION

1 tbsp olive oil
3 garlic cloves, crushed
5 fresh sage leaves
1 tbsp whole peppercorns
1 whole clove
4 portobello mushroom stalks
1 cup (250 mL) port wine (or red wine with 3 tsp
    brown sugar or agave nectar)
¼ cup (60 mL) balsamic vinegar
2 bay leaves

In a saucepan on medium-high, heat oil. Add garlic and sage and sauté for 1 minute. Add peppercorns, clove, and portobello stalks and sauté for 1 minute. Add wine, vinegar, and bay leaves and bring to a boil. Reduce heat to a high simmer for 15 minutes, until sauce has reduced slightly. Remove from heat, let cool, and strain, reserving sauce and discarding spices, garlic, and mushroom stalks. Reheat before serving.

HAZELNUT-CRUSTED PORTOBELLOS

2 tbsp balsamic vinegar
1 tbsp port wine
2 tsp tamari
1 tbsp olive oil
½ tsp liquid smoke
1 tsp Dijon mustard
1 tsp ground black pepper
1 tsp nutritional yeast
2 tbsp cornstarch
6 portobello mushrooms, stalks removed (reserve for
    use in port reduction)
3 garlic cloves, crushed
1 sprig fresh rosemary
⅔ cup (160 mL) finely chopped or crushed raw hazel
    nuts (a few pulses in a food processor works well)
1 tsp smoked salt

In a bowl, whisk together vinegar, port, tamari, oil, liquid smoke, mustard, pepper, yeast, and cornstarch. In a large freezer bag or plastic container with lid, place mushrooms, garlic, and rosemary. Pour in marinade and seal bag or container. Let sit for at least 30 minutes, or up to 2 hours.

Preheat oven to 375˚F (190˚C).

In a shallow bowl, add hazelnuts. Take 1 mushroom at a time from the marinade and dip into hazelnuts, making sure each is well-coated. Place on a lightly oiled baking sheet. Sprinkle with smoked salt before placing in oven. Bake for 12 minutes, turn mushrooms over, then bake for another 12–13 minutes, until hazelnuts are toasted and mushrooms are cooked.

CARAMELIZED FENNEL PARSNIP MASH

10 parsnips, trimmed and peeled
1 garlic bulb, cloves separated
2 tbsp olive oil
½ tsp salt
2 tbsp grapeseed oil
1 large fennel bulb or 2 small, trimmed
    and sliced thinly, lengthwise
½ tsp salt
½ tsp balsamic vinegar
1-3 tbsp olive oil
1-3 tbsp unsweetened milk (nut, rice, etc.)
½ tsp ground black pepper
½ tsp cayenne pepper (optional)
salt, to taste

Preheat oven to 375˚F (190˚C).

Place parsnips in a glass baking dish or into aluminum foil packets with about 2 parsnips per packet, along with 2 or 3 garlic cloves. Rub parsnips and garlic with 2 tbsp olive oil and sprinkle with salt. Tightly close packets or cover baking dish with foil and bake for 25-40 minutes, or until parsnips are soft.

Meanwhile, in a frying pan on medium, heat grapeseed oil. Add fennel and sauté for 1 minute. Season with salt, cover, and cook for 5 minutes. Stir fennel and cover for another 5 minutes. Add vinegar and cook for another 5 minutes or so until fennel is lightly caramelized and getting soft. Remove from heat.

Roughly chop cooked parsnips and add to large heat-proof bowl or pot, along with garlic and any reserved oil. Add 1–3 tbsp olive oil, milk, pepper, and cayenne and, using a potato masher or immersion blender, mash until smooth. Add more milk if mixture is too thick. Stir in caramelized fennel and season with salt to taste.

TO PLATE:

Cut each mushroom in half and place in the middle of a rectangular plate. Spoon 2 tbsp of port sauce over mushrooms. Place ⅓ cup (80 mL) of parsnip mash on 1 side and 1 tbsp of marmalade on the other.

LEEK & OYSTER MUSHROOM RISOTTO CAKES WITH YELLOW BEET REDUCTION

A different way to serve a classic risotto. The oyster mushrooms give a slight seafood flavor to the dish.

• **MAKES 6–8 SERVINGS.**

LEEK & OYSTER MUSHROOM RISOTTO CAKES

4–5 cups (1–1.25 L) stock (p. 45) or well-salted water
1 tbsp olive oil
2⅓ cups (550 mL) chopped and trimmed leeks
1 tsp salt
½ tsp ground black pepper
¼ tsp red pepper flakes
⅛ tsp kelp powder
¼ tsp dulse flakes
3 garlic cloves, minced
1½ cups (375 mL) trimmed and sliced oyster
   mushrooms
1⅔ cups (395 mL) arborio rice
⅓ cup (80 mL) dry white wine
1 tbsp olive oil
3 tbsp Cashew Cheese (optional, p. 192)
¼ cup (60 mL) rice flour
1 tbsp ground flax seeds
panko bread crumbs, for dredging
grapeseed oil, for frying

In a pot on medium-low, heat stock or water until just under a boil; keep at constant temperature.

Meanwhile, in a large pot on medium-high, heat 1 tbsp olive oil. Add leeks and sauté until softened. Add salt, pepper, red pepper flakes, kelp, dulse, and garlic. Add oyster mushrooms and continue to sauté until softened.

Add rice and stir constantly, cooking for 4 minutes, until rice becomes translucent. Add wine and continue to cook, stirring occasionally.

When wine has cooked off, add hot stock, 1 cup at a time, stirring constantly until stock is mostly evaporated and absorbed by rice before adding more. Reduce heat to medium; when you pause stirring, slow, lazy bubbles should rise to surface. Keep adding stock until rice is cooked and soft, about 20 minutes. Risotto should be a little thicker than a traditional one. Remove from heat.

Stir in 1 tbsp olive oil and Cashew Cheese and season with salt, to taste. Spread on an unoiled cookie sheet to let cool evenly.

In a large bowl, combine risotto with rice flour and flax. Form into 2-in (5-cm) wide, 1-in (2.5-cm) thick cakes. In a large frying pan on medium-high, heat a generous amount of grapeseed oil. Dredge top and bottom of each cake in shallow bowl of panko crumbs. Fry on each side for 5 minutes, or until golden.

Makes about 15 risotto cakes.

YELLOW BEET REDUCTION

1 tsp grapeseed oil
1 medium onion, chopped
1½ tsp salt
½ tsp cayenne pepper
1 tsp chopped fresh sage
¼ tsp chopped fresh thyme
3 tsp whole coriander seeds
2 cups cubed yellow beets
3 tbsp white wine vinegar
2 cups (500 mL) stock (p. 45)

In pot on medium, heat oil. Add onions and salt and sauté until onions are translucent. Add cayenne, sage, thyme, and coriander. Add beets and vinegar and cook for 4 minutes. Add stock and bring to a boil. Reduce heat and simmer, uncovered, for 20 minutes. In a blender, purée all ingredients until smooth. Be careful when blending hot liquids.

TO PLATE:

Spoon 2 tbsp of Beet Reduction on a plate. Place 2 Risotto Cakes on top.

PIPIÁN PESTO TORTELLINI WITH SEARED ASPARAGUS & ROASTED TOMATILLO SAUCE

Ever since I've been living in New York, I've been influenced by the abundance of Latin American foods found in grocery stores. This recipe is a result of that, filled with fresh, bright flavors. I use vegan wonton wrappers for the tortellini, which taste very similar to home-made vegan pasta, but are much less labor-intensive.

• **MAKES 4 SERVINGS AS A MAIN OR 6 APPETIZER PORTIONS.**

PIPIÁN PESTO TORTELLINI

1 tsp grapeseed oil
1 shallot, diced
3 garlic cloves, minced
⅓ cup (80 mL) pumpkin seed butter
1 tbsp lemon juice
¼–½ tsp salt, to taste
1 cup (250 mL) lightly packed fresh cilantro
1 cup (250 mL) lightly packed fresh parsley
¼ cup (60 mL) olive oil
1 13-oz (370-g) pkg round vegan wonton wrappers (approximately 64 wrappers)

In a small frying pan on medium, heat grapeseed oil. Add shallots and garlic and sauté until shallots are translucent. In a food processor or blender, blend shallots and garlic, pumpkin seed butter, lemon juice, salt, cilantro, and parsley. Slowly add olive oil to facilitate blending.

On a clean work surface, lay out a few wonton wrappers. Keep a small bowl of water nearby. Place 1 tsp filling in middle of each wrapper. With your finger or a small brush, dampen edges of each wrapper. Fold in half, pressing edges closed to seal. Dampen 1 corner of semi-circle and bring to center of tortellini; fold other corner over top. Squeeze gently to make sure corners stick together. Place on a parchment-lined cookie sheet and cover with damp tea towel or paper towel. Repeat with remaining filling and wrappers. (At this point, you can freeze the tray of tortellini, transferring to a freezer bag or container once frozen.)

Makes 28 tortellini.

Fill a large pot with well-salted water. Bring to a boil on high heat. Drop fresh or frozen tortellini into water and bring back to a boil. Cook for 2 minutes if fresh, 4 minutes if frozen. Tortellini will rise to top of water when done. Drain and set aside.

ROASTED TOMATILLO SAUCE

¾ lb (375 g) or 5 medium tomatillos, husks removed
4 unpeeled garlic cloves
2 tsp olive oil
¼ tsp salt
1 tbsp olive oil
¼ tsp fresh thyme

½ jalapeño pepper, seeded and chopped
¼ tsp salt
¼ tsp pepper
½ tsp agave nectar

Preheat oven to 325°F (160°C).
Rub tomatillos and garlic with 2 tbsp olive oil and sprinkle with ¼ tsp salt. Bake on an unoiled baking sheet for 20 minutes, until soft. Peel garlic. In a food processor or blender, process tomatillos and garlic with remainder of ingredients until smooth.

SEARED ASPARAGUS
2 tsp grapeseed oil
1 bunch asparagus, trimmed and sliced in half
    lengthwise, if very thick
salt, to taste

In a saucepan over medium-high, heat oil. Add asparagus and season with salt. Sauté for 2–4 minutes, until slightly browned and soft. Set aside

TO PLATE:
chopped fresh cilantro, to garnish
olive oil, to garnish

Toss tortellini with sauce. Portion into 4 shallow bowls (or 6, if serving as an appetizer). Place a few asparagus spears over top of pasta and garnish with chopped cilantro and olive oil.

COCONUT FETTUCINE ALFREDO WITH SEARED BRUSSELS SPROUTS & CHERRY TOMATOES

This is one of the first recipes I made when VSS started. It's rich and creamy, and by no means a traditional take on the original.

• MAKES 8–10 SERVINGS.

COCONUT FETTUCINE ALFREDO

1 lb (500 g) dry fettucine
1 tsp olive oil
2 tsp grapeseed oil
3 garlic cloves, minced
2 tsp minced sun-dried tomatoes
¼ tsp salt, (more, to taste)
½ tsp ground black pepper
¼ tsp red pepper flakes (optional)
1 tbsp tamari
2 tsp white wine vinegar
1 tbsp nutritional yeast
2 tbsp tahini
1 14-oz (398-mL) can coconut milk
1 tsp lime juice
salt, to taste

In a large pot, bring at least 4 qt (L) heavily salted water to a boil. Add pasta and olive oil and boil for 6–8 minutes, stirring occasionally and checking tenderness after 6 minutes. Drain in a colander.

Meanwhile, in a pot on medium-high, heat grapeseed oil. Add garlic, sun-dried tomatoes, salt, black pepper, and red pepper flakes and sauté for 1 minute. Add tamari, vinegar, nutritional yeast, and tahini. Slowly whisk in coconut milk. Reduce heat and bring to a slow simmer, whisking regularly. When simmering, add lime juice and season with salt, if needed. Remove from heat. Pour strained noodles back into pot and stir into sauce.

SEARED BRUSSELS SPROUTS & CHERRY TOMATOES

2 tsp grapeseed oil
20 Brussels sprouts, trimmed and cut in half lengthwise
20 cherry tomatoes, cut in half
1 tsp balsamic vinegar
salt and ground black pepper, to taste

In a large frying pan on high, heat oil. Add Brussels sprouts and sear, flat side down, for 3 minutes. Add tomatoes and balsamic vinegar. Season with salt and pepper and sauté for another 3 minutes.

TO PLATE:

Pile a portion of pasta in the middle of a shallow bowl. Spoon a few Brussels sprouts and tomatoes around the edges.

ROASTED GOLDEN BEET
& WILD ARUGULA PESTO PIZZA
WITH SESAME SHIITAKES & CASHEW CHEESE
ON A QUINOA CAULIFLOWER CRUST

This is my favorite gluten-free crust, with all of my favorite things on top, to create my other favorite thing: pizza.

• **MAKES 6–8 SERVINGS.**

MISO SESAME SHIITAKE MUSHROOMS (P. 190)

Follow instructions for this recipe, but do not dehydrate. These can be made first, and marinate while you prep the rest.

ROASTED GOLDEN BEETS

2 medium golden beets
2 tsp olive oil
½ tsp salt

Preheat oven to 375°F (190°C).

Wash beets and trim off tops and bottoms. Rub skins with oil and salt and wrap in aluminum foil. Bake for 35 minutes or until soft. When beets have cooled enough to handle, skin should just rub right off. Cut into slices or small cubes. Set aside.

WILD ARUGULA PESTO

4 garlic cloves
3 tbsp lemon juice
1 tsp salt
½ tsp ground black pepper
¼ tsp red pepper flakes
2 tbsp Cashew Cheese (p. 192)
3 cups (750 mL) washed and trimmed, lightly packed arugula (rocket)
3 cups (750 mL) lightly packed basil leaves
¼ cup (60 mL) olive oil

In a food processor or blender, purée garlic. Add lemon juice, salt, pepper, red pepper flakes, and Cashew Cheese. Add arugula and basil and continue to blend, slowly adding oil while blender is running.

Makes 1½ cups (375 mL).

QUINOA CAULIFLOWER CRUST

½ head cauliflower, roughly cut into large florets
2 tbsp olive oil
1 tsp tamari
1 medium red onion, diced
2 garlic cloves, minced
1 cup (250 mL) quinoa flour
1 tbsp cornstarch
1 tbsp ground flax seeds
2 tbsp nutritional yeast
1½ tsp salt
½ tsp red pepper flakes (optional)

Preheat oven to 375°F (190°C).

Fill a large pot with salted water and bring to a boil on high heat. Blanch cauliflower in boiling water for 3 minutes, until slightly soft but not over-cooked. Drain and set aside.

In a large bowl, combine cooked cauliflower with oil

and tamari. Mash using an immersion blender or place in a food processor and pulse until well-crumbled. (If using food processor, pour crumbled cauliflower into large bowl.) Add remainder of ingredients to bowl and combine well using a wooden spoon. Use your hands to form mixture into a sticky dough.

On a lightly oiled baking sheet, press dough into a circle or square, ¼-in (6-mm) thick. Bake for 10–15 minutes, until the edges are slightly golden. Set aside.

TO ASSEMBLE:

Cashew Cheese (p. 192)

Preheat oven to broil.

On pre-baked Quinoa Cauliflower Crust, spread a generous amount of pesto. Arrange beets and shiitakes evenly over crust. With a small spoon, scoop up Cashew Cheese; use another small spoon to pull small bits of cheese onto pizza. Broil for about 5 minutes, until shiitakes are roasted. Cut into rectangles or wedges.

WILD RICE DUMPLINGS
WITH PUMPKIN LEMONGRASS CURRY

The filling for these dumplings is also great when formed into patties for veggie burgers. You can use any vegetable you want in this curry: eggplant is quite good, as is tofu, bell peppers, or zucchini. The curry paste can be frozen in ice cube trays and used later (4 cubes per can of coconut milk).

• **MAKES 6–8 SERVINGS.**

WILD RICE DUMPLINGS

1 cup (250 mL) mixed uncooked wild, red,
    and brown rice
¼ cup (60 mL) uncooked red lentils
2½ cups (625 mL) stock (p. 45)
1 tsp tomato paste
2 tsp tamari
1 tsp almond butter
1 tsp grapeseed oil
1 medium shallot, diced
1 tsp finely grated fresh ginger
2 garlic cloves, finely chopped
1 tsp ground cumin
½ tsp ground coriander
¼ tsp ground cinnamon
½ cup (125 mL) chickpea flour
¼ cup (60 mL) chopped fresh cilantro
salt, to taste

In a large pot on medium-high heat, cook rice and red lentils, uncovered, in stock for about 20 minutes, stirring occasionally. When rice has absorbed enough water that water level is below rice, reduce heat to lowest setting, cover, and cook for 20 minutes. When rice is cooked, stir in tomato paste, tamari, and almond butter. Spread on an unoiled cookie sheet to cool evenly.

While rice cooks, in a pan on medium, heat oil. Add shallots, ginger, and garlic and sauté until shallots are translucent. Set aside to cool. In a large bowl, combine shallot mixture, rice, and lentils with cumin, coriander, and cinnamon. Add chickpea flour, stir in chopped cilantro, and season to taste with salt.

Preheat oven to 400°F (200°C).

Use ¼ cup (60 mL) of mixture to form round dumplings and place on an unoiled cookie sheet. Place about ½ tsp of coconut oil on each dumpling and bake for 10 minutes. Turn dumplings over and bake for another 10 minutes, until golden.

PUMPKIN LEMONGRASS CURRY

1 cup (250 mL) pumpkin purée
1 stalk lemongrass
¼ cup (60 mL) chopped shallots
1 large "thumb" ginger, grated
3 garlic cloves, chopped
1 tbsp coriander seeds (or 2 tsp ground)
1½ tsp cumin seeds (or 1 tsp ground)
½ tsp ground cinnamon
1–3 fresh Thai chilies, diced (or 1 tsp cayenne pepper)
1 tsp tomato paste
1 tsp tamari
1 tsp cane sugar
½ tsp salt
2 14-oz (398-mL) cans coconut milk

1½ cups (375 mL) quartered nugget potatoes
1 cup (250 mL) whole snap peas, ends trimmed

To make curry paste: In a sturdy blender or food processor, blend pumpkin purée, lemongrass (only if you are using a Vitamix blender; otherwise, set aside), shallots, ginger, garlic, coriander, cumin, cinnamon, chilies, tomato paste, tamari, sugar, and salt. If mixture is too thick, add 1 can coconut milk to curry paste. (You can freeze half now and use only ½ can of coconut milk when cooking.)

If making full recipe, add second can of coconut milk and blended curry paste to a saucepan over medium heat. If you didn't add lemongrass to paste, cut it into 4 or 5 large chunks and add it now. Simmer slowly for about 15 minutes. Reduce heat to low and add potatoes. Simmer until they are soft. Add peas and cook for about 5 minutes. Remove lemongrass stalks before serving.

TO PLATE:

2–3 tbsp fresh basil and/or cilantro chopped, for garnish

Ladle a serving of curry into a shallow bowl. Top with 3 dumplings and garnish with basil or cilantro.

MISO & JAPANESE EGGPLANT PIEROGIES WITH RAINBOW CARROT SHISO SLAW & COCONUT SOUR CREAM

Shiso is a fresh herb used in Japanese cooking. With distinct cinnamon, mint, and clove flavors and a slight savory spiciness, shiso is great in salads or cooked foods. I first made this recipe when catering a friend's wedding; her only request to me had been to incorporate shiso in the menu. She was happy with the result!

• MAKES 6–8 SERVINGS.

MISO & JAPANESE EGGPLANT PIEROGIES

For marinade:

¼ cup (60 mL) shiro miso

4 tsp grated fresh ginger

1 tbsp seasoned rice vinegar

1 tbsp orange juice

2 tsp agave nectar

1 tsp tamari

1 tbsp water

2 tsp sesame oil

2 tbsp grapeseed oil

1½ lb (750 g) Japanese eggplant or about 6 small or 3 large eggplants, halved

½ cup (125 mL) water

¼ cup (60 mL) chopped green onions

½ batch Pierogi Dough (p. 128) with 1 tbsp wasabi powder added when mixing flour and salt

Preheat oven to 425°F (220°C).

In a bowl, combine marinade ingredients. On an un-oiled baking sheet with rolled edges, arrange eggplant, cut sides up, and generously brush with marinade. Add ½ cup water to the sheet. Bake for 20–25 minutes, until eggplant is tender, turning eggplant over in last 5 minutes. Let cool on sheet.

Meanwhile, prepare Pierogi Dough and let sit, covered.

When eggplant is cool enough to handle, dice and place in a large bowl. Add any marinade liquids and stir in green onions.

Generously flour a clean work surface and knead dough for 2 minutes, adding more flour if necessary. Using ⅓ cup (80 mL) at a time, roll out with a floured rolling pin until ⅛-in (3-mm) thick. Use a pierogi maker or 3-in (8-cm) round cutter to cut circles. Place 2 tsp filling in center of each circle. Fold circle in half, smooth out any air bubbles, and pinch closed. If dough is too dry, dampen edges with water to seal. Place pierogies on a floured baking sheet. (At this point, you can freeze the pierogies on tray and transfer to a freezer bag or container once frozen.) You may leave them at room temperature or in the refrigerator for 1 hour before cooking.

Makes 25–30 pierogies.

To pan-fry fresh pierogies: Heat 1 tbsp grapeseed oil in a frying pan on medium. Add pierogies, flat side down, and cover pan. Cook for 1–2 minutes then turn over when golden. Cook other side for another 1–2 minutes, until golden.

For frozen pierogies, remove from freezer 5–10 minutes before cooking. Let each side cook for 3 minutes, covered, reducing heat if they start to brown too quickly.

GINGER SHISO DRESSING

1 tsp grated fresh ginger

1 garlic clove, finely diced or crushed

2 tbsp finely chopped fresh shiso

2 tsp finely chopped fresh cilantro

½ tsp Dijon mustard

2 tsp apple cider vinegar

1 tbsp seasoned rice vinegar

1 tbsp brown rice syrup

¼ tsp Sriracha (Thai hot sauce) (optional)

2 tsp nutritional yeast

¾ tsp toasted sesame oil

2 tsp olive oil

In a bowl, whisk all ingredients together until emulsified.

Makes ¼ cup (60 mL).

RAINBOW CARROT SLAW

1 bunch rainbow carrots, julienned

2 tbsp julienned fresh shiso leaves

In a bowl, combine Ginger Shiso Dressing, carrots, and shiso leaves.

TO PLATE:

Coconut Sour Cream (p. 195)

Pile ¼ cup (60 mL) carrot slaw in middle of a plate. Arrange 3–4 pierogies around slaw. Place 1 tbsp Coconut Sour Cream on side of plate.

SHERRY-ROASTED ROOT VEGETABLES ON BROWN RICE KALE PILAF WITH TAHINI BUTTER

A simple winter dish. The root vegetables can also be served on their own, topped with Shortcrust Pastry (p. 155) before baking, for a root-pot pie.

TAHINI BUTTER

2 tbsp tahini
2 tbsp lemon juice
1 roasted garlic bulb, skins removed
3 tsp tamari
1 tsp maple syrup
2 tbsp nutritional yeast
½ tsp Dijon mustard
¼ tsp cayenne pepper
¼ cup (60 mL) water
¼ cup (60 mL) olive oil

In a blender or food processor, blend all ingredients except oil. With blender running, slowly add oil until emulsified.

Makes 1 cup (250 mL).

SHERRY ROASTED ROOT VEGETABLES

¼ cup (60 mL) sherry
1 tbsp tamari
1 tsp lemon juice
1 tsp maple syrup
¼ tsp red pepper flakes
1½ tsp chopped fresh rosemary
¼ cup (60 mL) water
1 tsp cornstarch or 1½ tsp arrowroot powder
4 cups (1 L) cubed and peeled mixed squash,
    potatoes, sweet potatoes, turnips, rutabagas,
    parsnips, and beets, in any combination

Preheat oven to 425°F (220°C).

In a bowl, combine sherry, tamari, lemon juice, maple syrup, red pepper flakes, and rosemary. In a small bowl, whisk water and cornstarch together. Set aside.

In a large pot on medium-high heat, combine root vegetables and sherry mixture. Stir and cook for 3 minutes. Add cornstarch mix and continue to cook for another 3 minutes. Pour vegetables into a baking dish and cover with lid or aluminum foil. Bake covered for 20–25 minutes, until tender, then uncovered for 5 minutes.

BROWN RICE KALE PILAF

2 tsp grapeseed oil
1 medium shallot, sliced thinly
¼ tsp salt
3 cups (750 mL) tightly packed chopped kale
1 tsp tamari
2 cups (500 mL) cooked short grain brown rice
¼ cup (60 mL) Tahini Butter

In a large frying pan on medium, heat oil. Add shallots and salt and sauté until shallots are translucent. Add kale and tamari and stir for 1–2 minutes. Remove from heat.

In a large bowl, combine cooked rice with kale and add Tahini Butter. Stir to combine well.

TO PLATE:

3 tsp toasted sesame seeds
½ cup (125 mL) Tahini Butter

On a round shallow bowl or plate, place ⅓ cup (80 mL) pilaf. Spoon 2 tbsp Tahini Butter around rice. Add ½ cup (125 mL) root vegetables and top with a sprinkle of sesame seeds.

BREADS & GRAINS

- ALL-PURPOSE EVERYTHING DOUGH
- PIZZA DOUGH
- CRISPY FLATBREAD CRACKERS
- DARK HAZELNUT RYE BREAD
- HAZELNUT RYE CRISPS
- SOURDOUGH STARTER
- SOURDOUGH BREAD
- SWEET COCONUT BREAD
- PIEROGI DOUGH
- SESAME FLAX CRACKERS

ALL-PURPOSE EVERYTHING DOUGH

This versatile recipe will make 2 large pizza shells, 10 10-in (25-cm) crispy flat bread crackers, or 1 loaf of bread.

½ tsp maple syrup
1 cup warm (body temperature) water
1 tsp active dry yeast
2 tbsp olive oil
2–3 cups (500–750 mL) flour (most combinations of
    flour work great, e.g., 1 part rye, 3 parts spelt)
olive oil, to coat dough
see Dough Variations, next page

In a large bowl, mix maple syrup with warm water. Sprinkle with yeast, cover bowl, and set aside for 10 minutes until yeast blooms. Stir in oil, then slowly add flour, using a spoon at first, then switching to your hands. Knead dough for 10 minutes, until a smooth ball forms. Lightly coat ball with olive oil and place in a clean bowl. Cover with a towel and let rise in a warm, draft-free spot for 2 hours, until dough doubles in size.

To make bread, turn out dough onto a lightly floured surface. Knead a couple of times. Gently form into a loaf by tucking in sides of dough, forming a tight outside layer that helps loaf rise upright. Place loaf on a lightly floured or lightly cornmeal-covered baking sheet or pizza stone. Alternatively, you can place loaf into a lightly floured loaf pan. Cover with a tea towel and place in a draft-free spot for 1–2 hours, until loaf has doubled in size.

Preheat oven to 375°F (180°C).

If your oven runs a bit hot, brush top of loaf with water or milk before baking to prevent it from browning too quickly Bake for 45 minutes.

Add to dough when adding flour.

OLIVE

½ cup (125 mL) pitted and chopped kalamata olives

SUN-DRIED TOMATOES & BASIL

⅓ cup (80 mL) chopped sundried tomatoes and 2
   tbsp chopped fresh basil

SESAME

½ cup (125 mL) sesame seeds

PESTO

½ cup (125 mL) chopped basil
1 tsp lemon juice
⅓ cup (80 mL) chopped, toasted pine nuts
2 tbsp nutritional yeast
2 garlic cloves, finely chopped

BALSAMIC LAVENDER

1 tbsp dried lavender flowers (or fresh rosemary)
1 tsp ground black pepper
2 tsp balsamic vinegar

SWEET MUSTARD

1 tbsp grainy mustard or 2 tsp Dijon mustard
1 tbsp mustard seeds
1 tbsp brown rice syrup

LEMON PEPPER POPPY SEED

2 tsp lemon
rind of ½ lemon, grated
1 tsp ground black pepper
1 tbsp poppy seeds

PIZZA DOUGH

*The All-Purpose Everything Dough also makes a great
dough for pizza!*

1 recipe All-Purpose Everything Dough (p. 119)

Preheat oven to 375°F (190°C).

   Divide proofed dough in half. Turn out onto lightly
floured surface and knead for 5 minutes. Let rest for 30
minutes. Roll dough into a large circle or rectangle, 10-in
(25-cm) wide and ¼–½-in (½–1-cm) thick. Add toppings
of your choice and bake on a cornmeal-dusted baking sheet
or pizza pan for 20 minutes.

CRISPY FLATBREAD CRACKERS

You can make these crackers plain or you can add any of the variations below, which can be either brushed on top of the crackers or added to the plain dough when mixing in the flour. (See recipe photo, p.116.)

• **MAKES 10 10-IN (25-CM) CRACKERS OR ABOUT 80 SMALL CRACKERS.**

1 recipe All-Purpose Everything Dough (p. 119)
coarse sea salt, to taste

PESTO
¼ cup (60 mL) olive oil
2 tbsp nutritional yeast
3 tbsp chopped fresh basil
1 crushed garlic clove
1 tbsp lemon juice

BALSAMIC LAVENDER
¼ cup (60 mL) olive oil
2 tbsp balsamic vinegar
½ tsp pepper
1 tbsp dried lavender flowers (or fresh rosemary)

SWEET MUSTARD
¼ cup (60 mL) olive oil
1 tbsp grainy mustard
½ tsp apple cider vinegar
2 tsp brown rice syrup

GARLIC
¼ cup (60 mL) olive oil
2 tbsp nutritional yeast
2 garlic cloves, crushed
1 tsp lemon juice

Preheat oven to 425°F (220°C) and preheat an unoiled cookie sheet or cast iron griddle.

Divide proofed dough into 10 sections. Lightly oil rolling surface and rolling pin, then roll out each section to about 10-in (25 cm), ⅛-in (3-mm) thick. (Alternatively, roll out 2 tsp of dough into a 5-in [12-cm] long oval and cut into small cracker shapes.) Brush crackers with any of the above variations, or simply sprinkle with salt and pepper. Place on preheated cookie sheet. Bake for 3–5 minutes until slightly golden and crispy.

DARK HAZELNUT RYE BREAD

This dense, chocolaty rye bread is one of my favorites.

• MAKES 2 SMALL LOAVES.

1 tbsp maple syrup
2 cups (500 mL) warm water
2¼-oz (65-g) pkg yeast
2 tbsp olive oil
2 tbsp molasses
1 cup (250 mL) toasted hazelnuts
3 cups (750 mL) dark rye flour
2½ cups (625 mL) spelt or wheat flour
1 tbsp salt
olive oil, to coat dough

In a large bowl, mix maple syrup with warm water. Sprinkle with yeast, cover bowl, and set aside for 10 minutes until yeast blooms. Stir in olive oil, molasses, and hazelnuts, then slowly add flour and salt, using a wooden spoon at first then switching to your hands. Knead dough for 10 minutes until smooth ball forms, flouring your hands lightly if necessary. Lightly coat ball in olive oil and place in a clean bowl. Cover with a clean dish towel and let rise in a warm, draft-free spot for 2 hours, until dough doubles in size.

Preheat oven to 375°F (190°C).

Gently punch down dough and separate into 2 halves. Knead each ball a few times and form into loaves, cover with a cloth, and let rise for 1 hour. Bake each half in 9 x 5-in (2-L) loaf pan or on a lightly floured cookie sheet for 25–30 minutes.

HAZELNUT RYE CRISPS

Using the same recipe as for the rye bread, you can make crisps, which are amazing served with Cashew Cheese (p. 192) or paired with Beet & Cabbage Soup (p. 55).

• MAKES ABOUT 50 CRISPS.

1 recipe Dark Hazelnut Rye Bread (opposite)

Preheat oven to 375°F (190°C).

Slice baked, cooled loaf in half lengthwise, then into slices, as thin as you can make them, about ⅛-in (3-mm) thick. On an unoiled cookie sheet, bake for 5 minutes, turn slices over, then bake for another 5 minutes, until crisp.

SOURDOUGH STARTER

A starter can potentially keep forever if you take care of it; some bakeries have starters that are 100 years old. The older the starter gets, the more complex its flavors will be and the better it will taste. The grapes add a different kind fermentation to the mix, adding greater complexity of flavor.

½ cup (125 mL) organic grapes (optional)
½ cup (125 mL) organic whole wheat flour (rye and whole spelt flours also work)
1 cup (250 mL) water (room temperature, filtered)

Wrap grapes in cheesecloth to make a pouch, then crush grapes inside pouch.

In a 4-cup (1-L) glass jar or bowl, mix flour and water. Place crushed grapes (still inside cheesecloth pouch) in mixture. Keep in warm dark place. After 12 hours, discard ¼ cup (60 mL) of starter and add 2 tbsp new flour and 3 tbsp fresh water. Repeat every 12 hours for the first 48 hours.

On the third day, discard grapes. Starter is now ready to use. It should smell sweetly sour. If it smells "off" at any point, discard it and start again.

After using some of the starter to make Sourdough Bread (opposite), feed it with 2 tbsp flour and 3 tbsp fresh water. Store in a jar with a lid in refrigerator. Add 2 tbsp flour and 3 tbsp fresh water every 2 weeks to keep it fresh. To use after it's been refrigerated, add 3 tbsp flour and 2 tbsp water, and let sit, uncovered, for 12 hours or overnight in warm dark place.

SOURDOUGH BREAD

Sourdough is one of the oldest ways of making bread. A sourdough made in one location will taste differently from one made elsewhere. It's easy to double this recipe if you have enough starter. I usually slice one of them and keep it in the freezer so I always have bread for toast.

• MAKES 1 LOAF.

1 cup (250 mL) warm water
½ cup (125 mL) sourdough starter (opposite)
1½ tsp salt
2–3 cups (500–750 mL) flour, wheat mixed with 1 part whole wheat, spelt or rye
1 tsp olive oil
1 tbsp cornmeal

In a glass or ceramic bowl, mix water, starter, and salt. Slowly add flour, using a spoon at first then switching to your hands. Knead dough for 10 minutes until smooth ball forms. Dough should feel smooth and elastic and "alive," as gluten strands form, making dough stretchy. Lightly coat ball in olive oil and place in a clean glass or ceramic bowl. Cover with clean dish towel and keep in a warm, draft-free area for 12 hours, or overnight.

After 12 hours, dough should double in size. If not, let it rise for up to another 4 hours, if needed. Turn out dough onto lightly floured surface. Knead a few times and form into a loaf. Roll in flour. Place loaves on a baking pan sprinkled with cornmeal and cover with a clean dish towel. Let rise for 6 hours.

Preheat oven to 350°F (180°C).

With a sharp knife, make 2 slashes on top of loaf. Spray loaves with salted water (using a spray bottle) to keep crust from getting too hard during baking. Bake for 35 minutes, until bread is golden.

SWEET COCONUT BREAD

This bread pairs well with warmly spiced soups and curries, but is also a treat when eaten with just a little jam.

• MAKES 1 LOAF.

1 cup (250 mL) flaked unsweetened coconut, toasted
2 cups (500 mL) white spelt flour
1 tsp baking powder
1 tsp baking soda
½ tsp salt
¼ cup (60 mL) agave nectar or 8 Medjool dates, blended until smooth
¼ cup (60 mL) coconut oil, melted
2 cups (500 mL) rice milk
1 tsp lime juice
Smoke-Cured Coconut (p. 210) (optional, to garnish)

Preheat oven to 350°F (180°C).

In a bowl, whisk together dry ingredients. In a separate bowl, whisk together wet ingredients. Add wet ingredients to dry and combine with a wooden spoon until just mixed.

Add batter to a lightly oiled bread pan or preheated 8-in (20-cm) cast-iron pan. Sprinkle top of loaf with coconut flakes. Bake for 30–40 minutes, until a toothpick inserted in the center comes out clean.

Cool for at least 10 minutes before inverting out of pan.

SESAME FLAX CRACKERS

Top these crackers with Brazil Nut Sea Pâté (p. 31) or Cashew Cheese (p. 192) and a slice of tomato for a delicious raw snack.

• MAKES ABOUT 16 LARGE CRACKERS.

½ cup (125 mL) ground brown flax seeds
3 tbsp black sesame seeds
¾ cup (185 mL) water
1½ tsp tamari
¼ tsp salt
½ tsp sesame oil

In a bowl, combine all ingredients. Let sit for 3 hours or overnight.

On Silpat (non-stick) dehydrator trays, spread mixture ⅛-in (3-mm) thick. Dehydrate at 115°F (46°C) degrees for 15 hours, until crispy and dry. Break apart and store in a sealed container.

PIEROGI DOUGH

Use this with Miso Eggplant Pierogies (p. 112) or fill them with other savory fillings, or even fresh fruit and spices.

• MAKES 55–60 PIEROGIES.

3–4 cups (750 mL–1 L) white spelt flour
1 tsp salt
1¼ cups (310 mL) water
⅓ cup (80 mL) grapeseed or olive oil

In a large bowl, mix flour and salt. Stir in water and oil until a sticky dough forms. Cover bowl and let rest for 30 minutes. Generously flour a clean work surface. Turn out dough and knead for 2 minutes, adding more flour if necessary.

Using ⅓ cup (80 mL) dough at a time, roll out with a floured rolling pin until ⅛-in (3-mm) thick. Use a pierogi maker or 3-in (8-cm) round cutter to cut circles. Place 2 tsp filling in center, then fold dough circle in half. Smooth out any air bubbles, then pinch edges to seal. If dough is too dry, dampen edges with a little water. Place pierogies on a floured baking sheet. (At this point,

you can freeze pierogies on the tray and transfer to freezer bag or container once frozen.) You can leave them at room temperature or in refrigerator for 1 hour before cooking.

To cook fresh pierogies, bring a large pot of water to boil on high heat. Reduce heat to medium-high and drop pierogies in, being careful not to crowd pot. Let cook for 3 minutes, and remove with a strainer or sieve.

To cook frozen pierogies, remove from freezer when heating water and let sit for at least 5 minutes before cooking. Boil for 5 minutes. Strain.

To pan-fry fresh pierogies, heat 1 tbsp grapeseed oil in a frying pan on medium heat. Add pierogies, flat side down, and cover pan. Cook for 1–2 minutes and turn when golden. Cook for another 1–2 minutes, until golden.

To pan-fry frozen pierogies, remove from freezer 5–10 minutes before cooking. Let each side cook for 3 minutes, reducing heat if they start to brown too quickly.

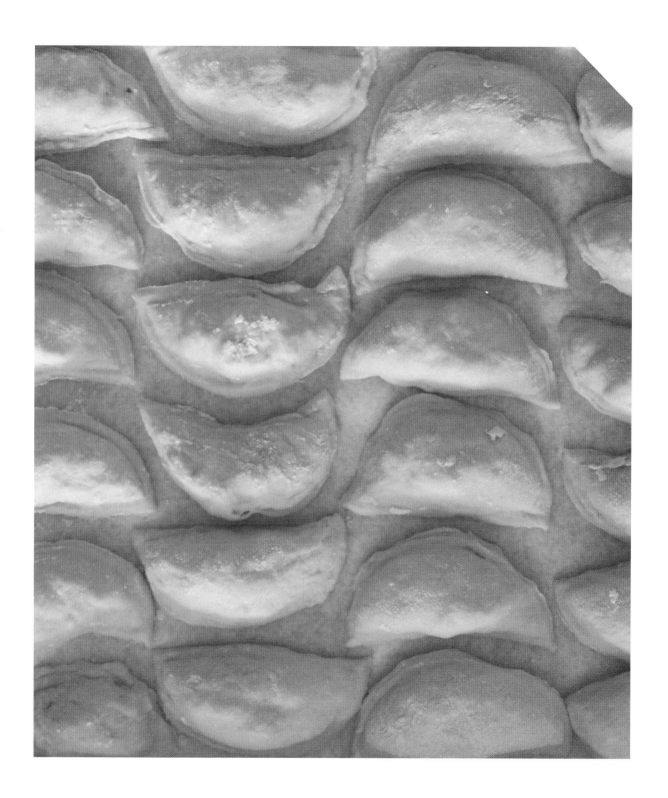

DESSERTS

- DARK CHOCOLATE CAKE WITH CHOCOLATE GANACHE GLAZE & AVOCADO MINT ICE CREAM
- WHITE CHOCOLATE CASHEW MOUSSE WITH DATE CARAMEL & CARDAMOM
- GRAHAM SHORTCAKES WITH FRESH BERRIES, HAZELNUT ICE CREAM
  & VANILLA CASHEW CREAM
- FIG MAPLE PECAN PIE WITH COCONUT LEMON ICE CREAM
- CHOCOLATE HAZELNUT PIE WITH BALSAMIC CHOCOLATE SAUCE
  & LAVENDER VANILLA ICE CREAM
- PUMPKIN MOUSSE PIE WITH CARAMEL & CARDAMOM ALMOND ICE CREAM
- ANCHO CHOCOLATE TRUFFLE PIE WITH SEA SALT
  & BUTTERNUT SQUASH WALNUT ICE CREAM
- CARROT CAKE WITH CARAMELIZED FIGS, PISTACHIO ICE CREAM & CACAO NIBS
- COCONUT PINEAPPLE CREAM PIE
- CASHEW LEMON PUDDING CAKE
- PEANUT BUTTER, WHITE CHOCOLATE & BROWNIE CHEESECAKE
- PUMPKIN MAPLE CINNAMON BUNS
- SWEET POTATO LIME CRÈME BRÛLÉE
- SALTED RYE SABLÉS
- TOASTED NUT SABLÉS
- CANDIED GINGER DATE COOKIES
- SHORTCRUST PASTRY
- COCONUT PASTRY
- NUT CRUST
- COCONUT RICE CRUST
- CHOCOLATE OAT CRUST
- PEANUT OAT CRUST

DARK CHOCOLATE CAKE WITH CHOCOLATE GANACHE GLAZE & AVOCADO MINT ICE CREAM

This rich chocolate cake, with more chocolate on top, will pair beautifully with any ice cream, but I recommend creamy and refreshing Avocado Mint.

• MAKES 6–8 SERVINGS.

DARK CHOCOLATE CAKE
1 ½ cups (375 mL) flour
¼ cup (60 mL) cocoa powder
¼ cup (60 mL) brown sugar
2 tsp baking soda
½ tsp salt
1 cup (250 mL) water
⅓ cup soy yogurt or milk (or nut or rice milk)
2 tbsp orange juice
1 tbsp molasses
¼ cup (60 mL) maple syrup
¼ cup (60 mL) brown rice syrup
⅓ cup (80 mL) oil
1 tsp vanilla extract
2 oz (60 g) dark chocolate, melted

Preheat oven to 350°F (180°C).

In a bowl, combine dry ingredients and make a well in center. In a separate bowl, combine wet ingredients. Add wet ingredients to dry and stir until just mixed. Pour into a lightly oiled or non-stick 9-in (23-cm) cake pan and bake for 35–40 minutes or until a toothpick inserted in the center comes out clean. Let cool for 10 minutes and turn out onto a cooling rack.

CHOCOLATE GANACHE GLAZE
¾ cup (185 mL) coconut cream (you can refrigerate a can of coconut milk and use only the cream that separates to the top)
2 tbsp coconut oil
1 cup (250 mL) chocolate chips or shavings
2 tbsp brown rice syrup
2 tbsp maple syrup
1 tsp vanilla extract
2 tbsp cocoa powder

In a pot on medium heat, add coconut milk, oil, and chocolate chips, stirring constantly until melted. Add syrups, vanilla extract and cocoa powder. Spoon or pour over the cooled cake, and refrigerate, or let sit until the glaze hardens. Alternatively, you can serve the cake as is, and spoon warm glaze on top just before serving.

Makes enough for 1 10-in (25-cm) cake.

TO PLATE:
Avocado Mint Ice Cream (p. 165)
Portion a slice of cake on a small plate. Top with 1 scoop ice cream.

WHITE CHOCOLATE CASHEW MOUSSE WITH DATE CARAMEL & CARDAMOM

Vegan white chocolate, you say? This dessert is rich and full of cocoa butter flavor, and the sweetness of the mousse and caramel are a perfect match with the bitter cacao nibs and spicy cardamom.

• **MAKES 6 SERVINGS.**

WHITE CHOCOLATE CASHEW MOUSSE

⅓ cup (80 mL) coconut oil
1.4 oz (40 g) cocoa butter
2 cups (500 mL) raw cashews, soaked in 2 cups water overnight and drained
1 14-oz (398-mL) can coconut milk
½ cup (125 mL) maple syrup
3 tbsp coconut or rice flour
1 vanilla bean, scraped
½ tsp salt

In a double boiler on medium heat, melt coconut oil and cocoa butter and set aside. In a blender or food processor, purée cashews with coconut milk until smooth. Add maple syrup, flour, vanilla bean, and salt and blend until smooth. Slowly pour in cocoa butter and oil while blender is running and blend until smooth. Pour into a shallow pan, cover and refrigerate overnight.

DATE CARAMEL

6 dates, finely chopped
¼ cup (60 mL) brown rice syrup
¼ cup (mL) maple syrup
½ tsp salt

In a pot on medium heat, combine all ingredients and bring to a boil. Do not stir. Let boil for 2 minutes, then remove from heat. Let cool to room temperature.

Makes ½ cup (125 mL).

TO PLATE:

2 tsp cacao nibs
½ tsp cardamom seeds

With a mortar and pestle, grind cacao and cardamom. Sprinkle ¼ tsp across a plate. Scoop a serving of mousse on each plate and top with 2 tsp Date Caramel.

GRAHAM SHORTCAKES WITH FRESH BERRIES, HAZELNUT ICE CREAM & VANILLA CASHEW CREAM

A light summer dessert, slightly sweet.

• **MAKES 8–10 SERVINGS.**

VANILLA CASHEW CREAM

¾ cup (185 mL) cashews, soaked in 1 cup water overnight and drained
1 14-oz (398-mL) can coconut milk
⅓ cup (80 mL) maple syrup or agave
⅓ cup (80 mL) coconut oil
1 vanilla bean, scraped, or 1 tsp vanilla extract

In a blender, purée cashews with coconut milk and maple syrup on high until smooth and creamy. In a double boiler on medium heat, melt coconut oil. While blender is running, slowly add melted coconut oil and blend until incorporated and smooth. Stir in vanilla. Chill for at least 4 hours or overnight.

Makes 2 ½ cups (625 mL).

GRAHAM SHORTCAKES

1 cup (250 mL) white wheat or spelt flour
1 cup (250 mL) graham flour
1 tbsp baking powder
¾ tsp salt
½ cup (125 mL) coconut oil, room temperature
¼ cup (60 mL) light brown sugar
1 cup (250 mL) nut or rice milk
coarse salt, to garnish
sugar, to garnish

Preheat oven to 425°F (220°C).

In a food possessor, pulse flour, baking powder, salt, coconut oil, and sugar until crumbly and combined well. Transfer to a bowl and slowly add milk, stirring with a wooden spoon until a smooth dough forms, then use your hands, as needed. Turn dough out onto a lightly floured surface and, using a lightly floured rolling pin, roll out to ¾-in (2-cm) thick. Stamp out biscuits with a 1 ½-in (4-cm) cutter, brush with a little milk, and sprinkle with coarse salt and sugar. Bake for 15–20 minutes, or until golden.

Makes 10–12 shortcakes.

TO PLATE:

3 cups (750 mL) fresh seasonal berries
Hazelnut Ice Cream (p. 163)

Slice shortcakes in half. Place bottom half on plate and top with berries and dollop of Vanilla Cashew Cream. Top with other half of shortcake.

Graham Shortcakes with Fresh Berries, Hazelnut Ice Cream & Vanilla Cashew Cream, 135

Fig Maple Pecan Pie with Coconut Lemon Ice Cream, 138

FIG MAPLE PECAN PIE
WITH COCONUT LEMON ICE CREAM

Serve this pie slightly warm and gooey and enjoy its toasty pecan flavor.

• **MAKES 8–10 SERVINGS.**

FIG MAPLE PECAN PIE

2 cups (500 mL) coarsely chopped fresh black figs
1 cup (250 mL) coarsely chopped pecans
⅓ cup (80 mL) soy or almond milk
¼ cup (60 mL) coconut oil
juice of 1 lime
⅓ cup (80 mL) maple syrup
1 tbsp blackstrap molasses
3 tbsp flour (for gluten-free: coconut or rice flour),
   mixed with ¼ tsp baking soda and ½ tsp
   baking powder
1 tsp cocoa powder
½ tsp ground cinnamon
zest of 1 lime, finely grated
½ tsp salt

½ batch Shortcrust Pastry (p. 155), unbaked, set in a 10-in (25-cm) pie plate

Preheat oven to 425°F (220°C).

In a food processor, pulse figs and pecans until a small ball forms.

In a saucepan on low, heat milk and coconut oil until oil melts. Remove from heat and whisk in lime juice. Stir in maple syrup and molasses. Stir pecan mixture into milk mixture until well-combined.

In a separate bowl, combine dry ingredients. Fold into wet ingredients. Pour into uncooked pastry shell and bake for 15 minutes, then reduce oven temperature to 350°F (180°C) and bake for another 35–45 minutes, until set.

TO PLATE:

Coconut Lemon Ice Cream (p. 166)

Serve a slice of warm pie with a scoop of ice cream on the side.

CHOCOLATE HAZELNUT PIE WITH BALSAMIC CHOCOLATE SAUCE & LAVENDER VANILLA ICE CREAM

This recipe works best if you have a Vitamix blender to make the filling as smooth as possible, but you can also get good results with a food processor.

• MAKES 8–12 SERVINGS.

CHOCOLATE HAZELNUT PIE

¼ cup (60 mL) coconut oil
6 oz (175 g) chopped chocolate
½ cup (125 mL) raw cashews, in ½ cup water overnight and drained
¾ cup hazelnuts, toasted then soaked in ¾ cup water overnight and drained
10 oz (300 g) medium-firm tofu
⅓ cup (80 mL) maple syrup
10 Medjool dates, pitted
1 tsp vanilla extract
½ tsp ground cinnamon
½ tsp salt

1 recipe Nut Crust (p. 156); use hazelnuts and cinnamon

Preheat oven to 350°F (180°C).

In a double boiler on medium heat, melt coconut oil and chocolate, then set aside. In a Vitamix or food processor, blend remainder of filling ingredients until smooth. While blender is running, slowly pour in melted oil and chocolate and blend until smooth. Pour into a 10-in (25-cm) springform pan with pre-baked Nut Crust and bake for 25 minutes. Chill overnight.

BALSAMIC CHOCOLATE SAUCE

1 cup (250 mL) balsamic vinegar
¼ cup (60 mL) maple syrup
⅓ cup (80 mL) chopped dark chocolate (70 percent or higher cacao)

In a pot on medium heat, bring balsamic vinegar and maple syrup to a boil. Reduce heat and simmer for 10 minutes, or until reduced by half. Remove from heat and whisk in chocolate until melted.

Makes ⅔ cup (160 mL).

TO PLATE:

2 tbsp chopped hazelnuts
Lavender Vanilla Ice Cream (p. 165)

Place 2 tsp Balsamic Chocolate Sauce on plate. Place slice of pie on sauce and top with scoop of Lavender Ice Cream. Garnish with chopped hazelnuts.

PUMPKIN MOUSSE PIE
WITH CARAMEL & CARDAMOM
ALMOND ICE CREAM

Maybe I use pumpkin too much. Is it possible to use something that good too much? You tell me after trying this smooth and creamy take on the classic pumpkin pie; it's a bit like a cheesecake.

2 cups (500 mL) raw cashews, soaked in 4 cups water
   overnight and drained
1 cup (250 mL) baked, mashed sweet potatoes* (baked
   whole, wrapped in foil at 400°F [200°C] for 45
   minutes or until soft)
1 cup (250 mL) pumpkin purée
¼ cup (60 mL) molasses
½ cup (125 mL) maple syrup
1 tsp vanilla extract
2 tbsp almond butter
2 tbsp coconut flour
1 tsp ground cinnamon
¾ tsp ground ginger
¼ tsp ground allspice
¼ tsp ground nutmeg
⅛ tsp ground cloves
½ tsp salt
⅓ cup (80 mL) coconut oil, melted
½ batch Shortcrust Pastry (p. 155), pre-baked in a
   10-in (25-cm) springform pan or pie plate
or
Coconut Rice Crust (p. 156)

Preheat oven to 350°F (180°C).

In a food processor or blender, blend cashews, sweet potatoes, pumpkin, molasses, maple syrup, vanilla, butter, flour, spices, and salt until smooth. While blender is running, slowly add melted coconut oil. Pour into a 12-in (30-cm) springform pan with pre-baked crust and bake for 25 minutes.

*I use Hannah white sweet potatoes for a good texture, but Jewel or Garnet yams are also great.

CARAMEL

⅓ cup (80 mL) coconut oil
½ cup (125 mL) coconut cream
1 cup (250 mL) packed brown sugar
¼ cup (60 mL) brown rice syrup
½ tsp salt
1 tsp vanilla extract

In a pot on medium heat, bring all ingredients except vanilla to a boil, stirring only at the beginning to combine. Boil for 3 minutes without stirring or until temperature reaches 230°F (110°C) and remove from heat. Whisk in vanilla and let cool at room temperature.

Makes 1 cup.

TO PLATE:

Cardamom Almond Ice Cream (p. 167)

Spoon 2 tsp caramel in middle of a plate. Place a slice of pie on one side of Caramel and a scoop of ice cream on the other.

ANCHO CHOCOLATE TRUFFLE PIE WITH SEA SALT & BUTTERNUT SQUASH WALNUT ICE CREAM

This rich and velvety pie has just a slight hint of spice.

• MAKES 8–12 SERVINGS.

⅓ cup (80 mL) coconut oil
4 oz (115 g) chopped chocolate
1 cup (250 mL) raw cashews, soaked in 2 cups water
    overnight and drained
1 14-oz (398-mL) can coconut milk
⅔ cup (160 mL) cocoa powder
¾ cup (185 mL) maple syrup
3 tbsp coconut flour
1 tsp vanilla extract
¼ tsp ground cinnamon
⅛ tsp ground cloves
¼–½ tsp ancho or cayenne pepper, to taste
½ tsp salt
1 recipe Nut Crust (p. 156); use chocolate and walnuts

In a double boiler on medium heat, melt coconut oil and chocolate, and set aside. In a food processor or blender, blend remainder of filling ingredients until smooth. While blender is running, slowly pour in melted oil-chocolate mixture and blend until smooth. Pour into 10-in (25-cm) springform pan with pre-baked Nut Crust and chill overnight.

TO PLATE:

1 tsp ground cinnamon
Butternut Squash & Walnut Ice Cream (p. 166)
1 tsp flaked sea salt

Sprinkle a tiny pinch of cinnamon in a diagonal line across a square plate. Place a slice of pie in the middle and a scoop of ice cream beside it. Sprinkle a pinch of salt on top of pie before serving.

CARROT CAKE
WITH CARAMELIZED FIGS, PISTACHIO
ICE CREAM & CACAO NIBS

This dessert is full of natural sweetness from the dates and figs and features gentle autumn flavors.

CARROT CAKE

1⅓ cups (315 mL) spelt flour
¾ tsp baking soda
1 tsp baking powder
1 tsp ground cinnamon
1 tsp ground ginger
¼ tsp ground nutmeg
⅛ tsp ground cloves
⅛ tsp ground allspice
2 tsp cocoa powder
½ tsp salt
1 cup (250 mL) almond or rice milk
1 tsp apple cider vinegar
½ cup (125 mL) maple syrup
¼ cup (60 mL) oil
½ tsp vanilla extract
5 Medjool dates, pitted and chopped
⅔ cup (160 mL) grated carrots

Preheat oven to 350°F (180°C).

In a bowl, combine dry ingredients and make a well in the center. In a separate bowl, combine wet ingredients. Add dates and carrots. Add wet ingredients to dry, stirring until just mixed. Pour into a 9-in (25-cm) cake pan and bake for 20–25 minutes, or until a toothpick inserted in the middle comes out clean.

FIG CARAMEL

5 fresh black figs, thinly sliced
2 tbsp coconut oil
3 tbsp coconut milk
1 cup (250 mL) packed brown sugar
¼ cup (60 mL) brown rice syrup
½ tsp salt
1 tsp vanilla extract

In a pot on medium heat, bring all ingredients except vanilla to a boil, stirring only to combine. Boil for 3 minutes or until temperature reaches 230°F (110°C), and remove from heat. Whisk in vanilla. Let cool at room temperature.

TO PLATE:

Pistachio Ice Cream (p. 162)
1 tbsp cacao nibs

Place a slice of carrot cake onto each plate. Pour Fig Caramel over cake and top with a spoonful of Pistachio Ice Cream. Sprinkle a few cacao nibs around each plate.

COCONUT PINEAPPLE CREAM PIE

This flavorful and refreshing pie makes for a show-stopping dessert. Make this the day before you plan to serve it, because it needs an entire night to set properly.

• MAKES 6–8 SERVINGS.

2 14-oz (398-mL) cans coconut milk, chilled (use only cream that has separated out at top)
2 bananas (not over-ripe)
⅓ cup (80 mL) agave nectar
1 lime, juiced and zested
½ cup (125 mL) coconut oil, melted
1 cup (250 mL) pure pineapple juice
⅓ cup (80 mL) lemon juice
3 tbsp maple syrup
½ cup (125 mL) agave nectar
⅓ cup (80 mL) brown rice syrup
zest of 2 lemons, grated finely
3 tbsp arrowroot powder
1 tbsp agar agar powder
½ recipe Shortcrust Pastry (p. 155), pre-baked in 10-in (25-cm) springform pan or pie plate
or
1 recipe Coconut Rice Crust (p. 156)

In a blender or food processor, blend coconut cream, bananas, agave nectar, and lime juice and zest until smooth. While blender is running, slowly pour in coconut oil until emulsified. Pour into a bowl and refrigerate.

In a separate bowl, whisk together pineapple and lemon juice, maple syrup, agave nectar, brown rice syrup, lemon zest, and arrowroot powder. Pour into saucepan and sprinkle agar agar over top. Let sit for 2 minutes. On medium-low heat, bring pineapple mixture to a slight boil, stirring lightly but constantly. When little bubbles begin to form, remove from heat and promptly pour into cooled crust.

Chill pie for 2–3 hours in refrigerator. Spoon coconut filling into pie only after pineapple filling has set and coconut filling is firm enough to hold its shape. Chill overnight before serving.

TO PLATE:
Serve all by itself.

CASHEW LEMON PUDDING CAKE

This is probably the best cake in the whole world, so moist and flavorful (or so I've been told by the many people I've served it to at VSS). I like to serve it warm with a little Ginger-Infused Maple Syrup.

• MAKES 8–12 SERVINGS.

⅓ cup (80 mL) coconut milk
1 cup (250 mL) raw cashews, soaked in 2 cup water overnight and drained
juice of 1 lemon (about ¼ cup [60 mL])
½ cup (125 mL) agave nectar
¼ cup (60 mL) grapeseed oil
2 tbsp flour
½ tsp baking powder
½ tsp baking soda
1 cup (250 mL) maple syrup
zest of 1 lemon
juice of 1 lemon (about ¼ cup [60 mL])
1⅓ cups (315 mL) coconut milk
⅔ cup (160 mL) grapeseed oil
½ tsp vanilla extract
2½ cups (625 mL) flour
1 tsp baking powder
1 tsp baking soda
½ tsp salt

Preheat oven to 350°F (180°C).

In a blender or food processor, blend coconut milk with cashews, lemon juice, agave nectar, and oil. Pour into a bowl and gently whisk in flour, baking powder, and baking soda until just mixed. Set aside.

In a separate bowl, combine maple syrup, lemon zest, lemon juice, coconut milk, oil, and vanilla.

In another bowl, combine flour, baking powder and soda, and salt. Add maple syrup mixture and stir until just mixed. Pour into a 12-in (30-cm) springform pan. Gently pour blended cashew mixture onto cake in one layer. Fold batters together for a subtle marbled effect.

Bake for 45–60 minutes, until cashew mixture is set (cake should spring back if touched very lightly with a fingertip).

TO PLATE:

Place a slice of warm cake on each plate. Serve with Ginger-Infused Maple Syrup (p. 202).

PEANUT BUTTER, WHITE CHOCOLATE & BROWNIE CHEESECAKE

Everything that's decadent and delicious has gone into this one: white chocolate and peanut butter cheesecake marbled with dark chocolate brownie batter. (Note: If you've invited dinner guests, make sure they don't have peanut allergies!)

• MAKES 8–12 SERVINGS.

1.4 oz (40 g) cocoa butter
⅓ cup (80 mL) coconut oil
1 cup (250 mL) raw cashews, soaked in 2 cups
    water overnight and drained
⅔ cup (160 mL) coconut milk
½ cup (125 mL) maple syrup
½ cup (125 mL) peanut butter
1 tsp vanilla extract
½ tsp salt
⅔ cup (160 mL) white spelt flour
⅓ cup (80 mL) sugar
¼ cup (60 mL) cocoa powder
½ tsp baking soda
½ tsp baking powder
½ tsp salt
¼ cup (60 mL) white chocolate, chopped
½ cup (125 mL) soy milk
2 tbsp brown rice syrup
2 tbsp grapeseed oil
1 tbsp apple sauce
½ tsp apple cider vinegar

Preheat oven to 350˚F (180˚C).

In a double boiler, melt cocoa butter and coconut oil and set aside.

In a blender or food processor, blend cashews, coconut milk, maple syrup, peanut butter, vanilla extract, and ½ tsp salt. While blender is running, slowly pour in melted coconut oil and cocoa butter and process until smooth.

In a separate bowl, combine flour, sugar, cocoa powder, baking soda and powder, and ½ tsp salt. Make a well in the center.

In a double boiler, melt chocolate. Whisk in 1 tbsp of soy milk at a time to temper chocolate. Whisk in brown rice syrup, oil, apple sauce, and cider vinegar.

Gently stir the chocolate mixture into dry ingredients, but do not over-mix. Alternating chocolate batter and peanut butter white chocolate batter, spoon into a lightly oiled 10-in (25-cm) springform pan. Use a knife to marble cake. Bake for 30 minutes or until toothpick inserted into the brownie part of the cake comes out clean.

TO PLATE:
Serve this all by itself.

PUMPKIN MAPLE CINNAMON BUNS

Less sweet than regular cinnamon buns, but just as gooey and irresistible.

• **MAKES 10–12 BUNS.**

1 cup (250 mL) warm water or milk (nut, rice, etc.)
1 tbsp molasses
¾ tsp yeast
⅓ cup (80 mL) puréed pumpkin
½ tsp salt
2 tbsp grapeseed oil
1 tsp ground cinnamon
1 tsp ground ginger
¼ tsp ground nutmeg
⅛ tsp ground cloves
3 cups (750 mL) spelt flour, plus ¾ cup (185 mL) for kneading
1 tsp grapeseed oil
8 Medjool dates
½ cup (125 mL) maple syrup
¼ cup (60 mL) brown sugar
2 tsp ground cinnamon
⅓ cup (80 mL) softened coconut oil or softened Earth Balance vegan margarine
⅓ cup (80 mL) chopped pecans (optional)

In a bowl, add water or milk and molasses and stir to combine. Sprinkle yeast on top, cover bowl, and set aside for 5–10 minutes, until yeast has bloomed.

Stir in pumpkin, salt, 2 tbsp oil, and ground spices. Slowly add flour, ½ cup (125 mL) at a time, until a workable dough forms. Switching to your hands, turn out dough onto a lightly floured surface. Knead dough for 5–10 minutes, until a smooth ball forms. In a clean bowl, lightly coat dough with 1 tsp oil. Cover bowl with a tea towel and set aside in a warm, draft-free spot and let rise for 2 hours, until doubled in size.

Meanwhile, in a blender or food processor, blend dates with maple syrup, sugar, cinnamon, and coconut oil or vegan margarine. Set aside.

When dough has risen, turn out onto a lightly floured surface. Pull or roll out into a ½-in (1-cm) thick rectangle. Spread ⅔ of date filling over dough, then sprinkle with pecans. Roll up into a cylinder and cut into 1 ½-in (4-cm) slices. In a lightly oiled 10 x 12-in (25 x 30-cm) glass baking pan, place buns, spaced evenly. Top with the remaining date mixture. Cover and let rise for 35 minutes.

Preheat oven to 325°F (160°C). Bake for 20–25 minutes, until toothpick inserted into center of a bun comes out clean. Serve warm.

TO PLATE:
Serve with Vanilla Cashew Cream (p. 135) and Spiced Maple Syrup (p. 202).

SWEET POTATO LIME CRÈME BRÛLÉE

This is probably the most sought-after recipe from VSS; I almost hesitated to put it in this book! But here it is, with its sweet potato secret revealed. Make this the day before you plan to serve; it needs to chill overnight.

• MAKES 6–8 SERVINGS.

2–3 small white-fleshed Hannah sweet potatoes (enough to yield 2 cups/500 mL when cooked and mashed)
1 13-oz (370-g) can coconut milk
2 tbsp lime juice
1 tsp lime zest
1 vanilla bean, scraped, or 1 tsp vanilla extract
3 tbsp maple syrup
¼ cup (60 mL) cane sugar, for sprinkling

Preheat oven to 375°F (190°C).

Bake whole sweet potatoes on a baking sheet, wrapped in foil, for 45 minutes–1 hour, or until soft. Let cool and then peel. Add 2 cups (250 mL) sweet potatoes to a blender or food processor. Add coconut milk, lime juice and zest, vanilla, and maple syrup and blend until smooth. Chill for 6 hours, or overnight.

Spoon into crème brûlée cups. Sprinkle a layer of sugar a scant ⅛-in (3-mm) thick over crème. Using a food torch, caramelize sugar so a smooth hard crust forms.

SALTED RYE SABLÉS

The texture of these is very much like shortbread and the taste is perfect for a refined sweet tooth, with just a hint of sweetness. Topped with sesame seeds, these sablés are a perfect mate for Cashew Cheese (p. 192).

• **MAKES ABOUT 24 COOKIES.**

1 ¼ cups (310 mL) rye flour
4 tbsp arrowroot powder
½ tsp salt
½ cup (125 mL) softened coconut oil
4 tbsp maple syrup or agave nectar
½ tsp lemon juice
¼ tsp sea salt, for sprinkling

In a bowl, combine flour, arrowroot powder, and salt. Using a pastry cutter or fork, cut in softened coconut oil. Switch to your hands and completely blend oil and flour, until a crumbly dough forms. Add maple syrup and lemon juice and combine well.

Turn dough out onto a large piece of plastic wrap and form into a 2-in (5-cm) thick log. Wrap dough in plastic wrap and refrigerate for 20 minutes.

Preheat oven to 350˚F (180˚C).

Unwrap dough and, with a sharp knife, slice into ¼-in (6-mm) thick slices. Place on an un-oiled cookie sheet, 1 in (2.5 cm) apart. Lightly sprinkle tops of cookies with sea salt. Bake for 12–15 minutes. Transfer to a cooling rack to cool completely.

TOASTED NUT SABLÉS

I like to use pecans or pistachios in these cookies, which are a slightly different take on Rye Sablés (p. 153), and a tiny bit sweeter.

• MAKES ABOUT 30 COOKIES.

¾ cup (185 mL) rice flour
1 cup (250 mL) rye flour
4 tbsp arrowroot powder
¼ tsp salt
⅔ cup (160 mL) softened coconut oil
½ cup (125 mL) chopped nuts (pecans or pistachios)
5 tbsp maple syrup
½ tsp lemon juice

In a bowl, combine rice and rye flour, arrowroot powder, and salt. Using a pastry cutter or fork, cut in softened coconut oil. Switch to your hands and completely blend oil and flour, until a crumbly dough forms. Add nuts, maple syrup, and lemon juice and combine well.

Turn dough out onto a large piece of plastic wrap and form into a 2-in (5-cm)-thick log. Wrap dough with plastic wrap and refrigerate for 20 minutes.

Preheat oven to 350°F (180°C).

Unwrap dough and, with a sharp knife, slice into ¼-in (6-mm) thick slices. Place on an unoiled cookie sheet ¼-in (6-mm) apart. Bake for 12–15 minutes. Transfer to a cooling rack to cool completely.

CANDIED GINGER DATE COOKIES

These are chewy rather than crispy ginger cookies, and extra spicy.

• MAKES ABOUT 24 COOKIES.

1½ cups (375 mL) spelt flour
½ tsp baking powder
½ tsp baking soda
½ tsp salt
1 tsp ground ginger
½ tsp ground nutmeg
¼ tsp ground cloves
¼ cup (60 mL) molasses
¼ cup (60 mL) brown rice syrup
½ cup (125 mL) sunflower oil
1 tsp apple cider vinegar
1 tsp vanilla extract
8 Medjool dates, pitted and chopped
¼ cup (60 mL) chopped candied ginger

Preheat oven to 350°F (180°C).

In a bowl, combine dry ingredients. In a separate bowl, combine wet ingredients with dates and candied ginger. Pour the wet ingredients into dry and gently combine until well-mixed.

Take 2 tsp dough and form into a ball. Place on an un-oiled cookie sheet, 2-in (5-cm) apart. Repeat with remaining dough. Gently press a fork onto cookies to flatten slightly. Bake for 12–15 minutes, until edges are slightly golden. Transfer to a cooling rack to cool completely.

SHORTCRUST PASTRY

This versatile pastry freezes well; just wrap the dough in a couple layers of plastic wrap. To defrost, leave in refrigerator overnight.

• **MAKES ENOUGH FOR 2 10-IN (25-CM) COVERED PIES OR 4 SHELLS.**

3 cups (750 mL) white spelt flour
½ tsp salt
¾ cup (185 mL) vegetable shortening
¼ cup (60 mL) Earth Balance vegan margarine
½ cup (125 mL) cold water

In a large bowl, sift flour and salt. With a pastry cutter or fork, cut in shortening and margarine until well combined. The mixture should be crumbly. Pour in cold water and stir to combine, using your hands at the end. Knead a few times until it forms a smooth dough. Make sure not to over-knead.

Generously flour a clean work surface. Portion dough into 4 parts. Form a ball with 1 part and gently flatten. Flour top of ball and turn it over a few times, flattening with your hand. Make sure it won't stick to work surface. Lightly flour a rolling pin and roll out dough to about ¼-in (6-mm) thickness. Fold in half, then lift and set onto pie plate. Unfold and press gently into place.

To blind bake crust, line with parchment paper, then pour in enough dried beans to cover bottom and bake at 350°F (180°C) for 10–12 minutes. Beans can be re-used.

COCONUT PASTRY

A beautiful pastry, a little less fatty than the Shortcrust (opposite), and made solely with coconut oil. It can be used in place of Shortcrust in any recipe.

• **MAKES 1 10-IN (25-CM) COVERED PIE OR 2 SHELLS.**

2 cups (500 mL) white spelt flour
½ tsp salt
½ cup (125 mL) softened coconut oil
1 tsp apple cider vinegar
⅓ cup (80 mL) cold water

In a large bowl, mix flour and salt. With a fork or pastry cutter, cut in coconut oil until well incorporated. Add vinegar and water and gently combine with a fork just until a dough forms. Use your hands, if needed.

Generously flour a clean work surface. Portion dough into 4 parts. Form a ball with 1 part and gently flatten. Flour top of ball and flip it over a few times, flattening with your hand. Make sure it won't stick to work surface. Lightly flour a rolling pin and roll out dough to about ¼-in (6-mm) thickness. Fold in half, then lift and set onto pie plate. Unfold and press gently into place.

To blind bake crust, line with parchment paper, then pour in enough dried beans to cover bottom and bake at 350°F (180°C) for 10–12 minutes. Beans can be re-used.

NUT CRUST

This is another no-fail, all-purpose crust. You can mix and match flavors to go with what you have on hand or the type of pie you're making—almond cinnamon crust, hazelnut mocha crust, or chocolate walnut crust are good choices.

• **MAKES 1 10-IN (25-CM) CRUST.**

1 cup (250 mL) nuts (almonds, hazelnuts, or
    walnuts), ground
¾ cup (185 mL) spelt flour (for gluten-free: ¾ cup
    rice flour + 1 tbsp arrowroot powder or corn
    starch)
1 tsp cocoa powder (or 1 tsp ground cinnamon, or
    1 tsp fine ground coffee + 1 tsp vanilla extract)
½ tsp salt
2 tbsp grapeseed oil
2 tbsp brown rice syrup
½ tsp apple cider vinegar
½ tsp flavored extract, optional (almond, vanilla,
    orange, etc.)

Preheat oven to 350°F (180°C).

In a bowl, combine nuts with dry ingredients and make a well. In a separate bowl, combine wet ingredients. Add wet ingredients to dry and stir until combined. Use your hands, as needed, at the end to combine ingredients. Press into a pie plate or 10-in (25-cm) springform pan.

COCONUT RICE CRUST

This crust has a shortbread taste and is a great gluten-free option that goes with almost any pie filling.

• **MAKES 1 10-IN (25-CM) CRUST.**

1 cup (250 mL) finely shredded unsweetened coconut
½ cup (125 mL) rice flour
2 tbsp cornstarch
½ tsp salt
2 tbsp brown rice syrup
2 tbsp grapeseed oil

Preheat oven to 350°F (180°C).

In a bowl, combine dry ingredients and make a well. Add syrup and oil and stir until combined. Use your hands, as needed, at the end to combine ingredients. Press into a pie plate or 10-in (25-cm) springform pan. Bake for 10 minutes, until lightly golden.

CHOCOLATE OAT CRUST

This simple crust goes great with most fillings.

• **MAKES 1 10-IN (25-CM) CRUST.**

¾ cup (185 mL) rolled oats
1 cup (250 mL) spelt flour (for gluten-free: 1 cup rice
   flour plus 1 tbsp arrowroot powder or cornstarch)
2 tbsp cocoa powder
½ tsp salt
3 tbsp grapeseed oil
3 tbsp brown rice syrup or agave nectar

In a bowl, combine dry ingredients and make a well. Add oil and brown rice syrup and stir until combined. Use your hands, as needed, at the end to combine ingredients. Press into a pie plate or 10-in (25-cm) springform pan.

PEANUT OAT CRUST

Peanuts are always a good fit for chocolate. I don't use peanut butter in any VSS cooking due to potential allergy issues, but I do enjoy this myself. (You can also substitute another nut butter, such as almond, cashew, etc.)

• **MAKES 1 10-IN (25-CM) CRUST.**

1 cup (250 mL) oat flour (process 1¼ cups [310 mL]
   rolled oats in a food processor)
½ cup (125 mL) rolled oats
3 tbsp peanut butter (or other nut butter)
2 tbsp maple syrup
2 tbsp oil

Preheat oven to 350°F (180°C).
   Combine flour and oats and make a well. In a separate bowl, combine nut butter, maple syrup, and oil. Add wet ingredients to dry and stir until combined. Use your hands, as needed, at the end to combine ingredients. Press into a pie plate or 10-in springform pan.

ICE CREAMS

- DARK CHOCOLATE ALMOND ICE CREAM

- PISTACHIO ICE CREAM

- HAZELNUT ICE CREAM

- AVOCADO MINT ICE CREAM

- LAVENDER VANILLA ICE CREAM

- COCONUT LEMON ICE CREAM

- BUTTERNUT SQUASH & WALNUT ICE CREAM

- CARDAMOM ALMOND ICE CREAM

- BALSAMIC MARBLED COCONUT ICE CREAM

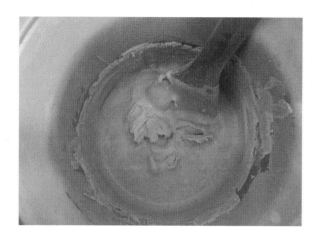

ICE CREAM

If you have an ice cream maker, you can freeze the following ice cream recipes according to the manufacturer's directions. Even if you don't own one, you can still make perfect ice cream. Here is my method:

Take two metal bowls that nest together well. Fill one up with water and place the other one on top. (You may want to do this in the sink, as adjusting the water levels can be messy.) Weigh the top bowl down with a bag of frozen peas, until the bowls are nesting with an even layer of water between them. Place the stacked bowls in the freezer for two hours, until water is frozen solid.

Remove bag of peas. Pour the well-chilled ingredients into your frozen bowl and stir it. It will start freezing to the bowl as you scrape the sides. Stir for at least five minutes before taking a break. You can put the bowl back in the freezer for about ten minutes to harden the ice cream slightly and keep the bowl frozen, then remove it and stir again, until ice cream reaches the desired consistency. Transfer ice cream to a sealed container and keep in the freezer for up to two weeks.

The base in most of these recipes is coconut milk. You can substitute other milks, but coconut milk will result in a smoother and creamier ice cream, especially when turning by hand, because of its higher fat content.

DARK CHOCOLATE ALMOND ICE CREAM

You can make this without the chopped almonds, but their crunch complements the creamy, rich ice cream.

• MAKES 2 CUPS (500 ML).

½ cup (125 mL) almonds, soaked in ½ cup water overnight and drained
1 cup (250 mL) coconut milk
⅓ cup (80 mL) maple syrup
3 tbsp cocoa powder
½ tsp almond extract (optional)
1 tbsp melted coconut oil
¼ cup (60 mL) chopped dark chocolate, melted
1 vanilla bean, scraped, or 1 tsp vanilla extract
¼ cup (60 mL) finely chopped almonds (optional)

In a blender or food processor, purée all ingredients, except final ¼ cup chopped almonds, until smooth. Stir in chopped almonds. Chill in a covered bowl or container in refrigerator overnight before following manufacturer's instructions for ice cream maker, or those provided on p. 161.

PISTACHIO ICE CREAM

Creamy and rich with a toasty pistachio flavor, a little like kulfi, a dense type of ice cream from India.

• MAKES 3 CUPS (750 ML).

½ cup (125 mL) pistachios, toasted, then soaked in 1 cup water overnight and drained
½ cup (125 mL) cashews, soaked in 1 cup water over night and drained
1 14-oz (398-mL) can coconut milk
⅓ cup (80 mL) maple syrup
1 vanilla bean, scraped, or ½ tsp vanilla extract
¼ tsp salt

In a blender or food processor, purée all ingredients until smooth. Chill in a covered bowl or container in the refrigerator overnight before following manufacturer's instructions for ice cream maker, or those provided on p. 161.

HAZELNUT ICE CREAM

There is an amazing organic hazelnut farm in rural Agassiz, BC, where I get all my hazelnuts. Then I have to stop myself from putting hazelnuts in everything I make! Except this wonderful ice cream.

• **MAKES 2⅓ CUPS (550 ML).**

1 14-oz (398-mL can coconut milk
¼ cup (60 mL) agave syrup
¼ cup (60 mL) maple syrup
⅛ tsp guar gum
1 vanilla bean, scraped, or 1½ tsp vanilla extract
¼ cup (60 mL) toasted and skinned hazelnuts, soaked
**   in 1 cup water overnight and drained**
3 tbsp chopped toasted hazelnuts

In a pot on medium heat, bring coconut milk, agave syrup, and maple syrup to just under a boil. Whisk in guar gum and stir until mixture starts to thicken. Let cool. Stir in vanilla.

In a blender or food processor, purée soaked hazelnuts with coconut milk mixture. Stir in chopped hazelnuts. Chill in a covered bowl or container in the refrigerator overnight before following manufacturer's instructions for ice cream maker, or those provided on p. 161.

Lavender Vanilla Ice Cream, opposite

AVOCADO MINT ICE CREAM

Avocado lends a smooth, creamy texture and a beautiful color to this unusual ice cream.

• MAKES 2½ CUPS (625 ML).

1 14-oz (398-mL) can coconut milk
¼ cup (60 mL) agave syrup
¼ cup (60 mL) brown rice syrup
1 tbsp lime juice
1 avocado
1 cup (250 mL) fresh mint leaves

In a blender or food processor, blend all ingredients until smooth. Chill in a covered bowl or container in the refrigerator for at least 4 hours or overnight before following manufacturer's instructions for ice cream maker, or those provided on p. 161.

LAVENDER VANILLA ICE CREAM

The lavender flavor in this ice cream is subtle, with a hint of white chocolate.

• MAKES 2½ CUPS (625 ML).

1 14-oz (398-mL) can coconut milk
¼ cup (60 mL) agave syrup
¼ cup (60 mL) brown rice syrup
1 tbsp dried lavender flowers
¾ oz (25 g) cocoa butter
⅛ tsp guar gum
1 vanilla bean, scraped or 1½ tsp vanilla extract

In a pot on medium heat, bring coconut milk, agave syrup, brown rice syrup, and lavender to almost a boil. Add cocoa butter and guar gum, whisking until butter melts. Remove from heat. Let cool for 5 minutes. In a blender, purée until smooth. Stir in vanilla and chill in a covered bowl or container in the refrigerator overnight before following manufacturer's instructions for ice cream maker, or those provided on p. 161.

COCONUT LEMON ICE CREAM

Not as tart as a sorbet, this ice cream still delivers a clean palate-cleansing flavor.

• **MAKES 2⅔ CUPS (630 ML).**

1 14-oz (398-mL) can coconut milk
¼ cup (60 mL) sugar
¼ cup (60 mL) brown rice syrup
⅛ tsp guar gum
2 lemons, juiced and zested
¼ cup (60 mL) grated coconut (optional)

In a pot on medium heat, bring coconut milk, sugar, and brown rice syrup almost to a boil. Whisk in guar gum. Remove from heat, and stir in lemon zest, juice, and coconut. Chill in a covered bowl or container in the refrigerator overnight before following manufacturer's instructions for ice cream maker, or those provided on p. 161.

BUTTERNUT SQUASH & WALNUT ICE CREAM

Warmly flavored, a little like a pumpkin pie: this is real comfort-food ice cream.

• **MAKES 3 CUPS (750 ML).**

1 cup (250 mL) peeled and cubed butternut squash
¼ cup (60 mL) toasted walnuts
1 14-oz (398-mL) can coconut milk
½ cup (125 mL) maple syrup
½ tsp vanilla extract
¼ tsp ground cinnamon
⅛ tsp ground nutmeg

In a pot, place a 6-in (15-cm) vegetable steamer. Add at least 1-in (2.5-cm) water, place squash in steamer, and cover pot. Steam squash on medium-high heat for 10 minutes, until squash is tender. Set aside to cool.

In a blender or food processor, blend squash with remainder of ingredients until smooth. Chill in a covered bowl or container in the refrigerator overnight before following manufacturer's instructions for ice cream maker, or those provided on p. 161.

CARDAMOM ALMOND ICE CREAM

This is ice cream all grown up; earthy, bold, and light.

• **MAKES 2 CUPS (500 ML).**

½ cup (125 mL) blanched almonds, soaked in 1 cup
    water for 6 hours and drained
1 cup (250 mL) coconut milk
¼ cup (60 mL) maple syrup
2 tbsp brown rice syrup
1 tbsp olive oil
1 tsp vanilla extract
¼ tsp almond extract
1 tsp orange zest
½ tsp crushed cardamom seeds
⅛ tsp salt
1 tbsp finely chopped chocolate (optional)

In a blender or food processor, blend all ingredients until smooth. Chill in a covered bowl or container in the refrigerator overnight before following manufacturer's instructions for ice cream maker, or those provided on p. 161.

BALSAMIC MARBLED COCONUT ICE CREAM

This ice cream is great with Dark Chocolate Cake (p. 133) or Chocolate Hazelnut Pie (p. 139).

• **MAKES 2½ CUPS (625 ML).**

1 14-oz (398-mL) can coconut milk
¼ cup (60 mL) agave syrup
¼ cup (60 mL) brown rice syrup
¼ tsp guar gum
1 vanilla bean, scraped, or 1 ½ tsp vanilla extract
2 tbsp Balsamic Reduction (p. 205)

In a blender or food processor, blend all ingredients, except Balsamic Reduction, until smooth. Chill in a covered bowl or container in the refrigerator overnight before following manufacturer's instructions for ice cream maker, or those provided on p. 161.

After ice cream has been churned, gently fold in Balsamic Reduction. Do not over-mix at this point or you will lose the marbled effect. Transfer to a container and return to freezer if not serving immediately.

sept  VSS 23rd

GRAND MARNIER SPELT CREPES FLAMBÉ

~

PLAIN CREPES WITH CHOICES OF LEMON +
VANILLA BROWN SUGAR, PLUM COMPOTES,
MAPLE NUTS + SEEDS, GINGER INFUSED OR
SPICED MAPLE AND APPLE REDUCTION

~

PINEAPPLE ORANGE MIMOSA OR SPARKLING
$25

BRUNCH

- CRÊPES
- SWEET POTATO FRITTERS WITH COCONUT SOUR CREAM, APPLE TAMARIND CHUTNEY, ROASTED PINEAPPLE & SMOKE-CURED COCONUT
- PEANUT BUTTER OAT WAFFLES WITH WHITE CHOCOLATE MOUSSE & VANILLA PLUM COMPOTE
- PUMPKIN WAFFLES
- DOUBLE CHOCOLATE WAFFLES WITH MOCHA CREAM

CRÊPES

Classic crêpes are simple to make and great to eat with just a sprinkle of brown sugar and a squeeze of lemon. You can make them the day or night before and heat them back up in the pan; they will taste just as fresh.

• **MAKES ABOUT 6 CRÊPES.**

1 cup (250 mL) spelt or wheat flour
1 cup (250 mL) milk of your choice (nut, rice, etc.)
½ tsp salt
grapeseed or coconut oil or Earth Balance vegan
    margarine, for cooking crêpes

In a bowl or mixer, whisk or mix flour, milk, and salt. While blender is running or while continuing to beat batter, slowly add water, a little at a time, to make a smooth, thin batter. It should be thin enough to coat the back of a spoon but still drip off easily.

In a small, wide-bottomed, non-stick frying pan or griddle on medium, heat a scant tsp oil. Pour about ⅓ cup (80 mL) batter into middle of pan and lift and tilt pan so that crêpe thins and spreads to cover bottom of pan.

Cook until edges of crêpe begin to set, about 1 minute. Turn crêpe and cook other side for about 1 minute, until light golden brown. Stack crêpes on a plate and keep them warm in oven at minimum temperature with a damp cloth over them.

SWEET POTATO FRITTERS WITH COCONUT SOUR CREAM, APPLE TAMARIND CHUTNEY, ROASTED PINEAPPLE & SMOKE-CURED COCONUT

This is the first VSS brunch I ever served, and it's still one of my favorites. Leftover fritters (if there are any!) are great refried for a sandwich the next day.

• **MAKES 6–8 SERVINGS.**

SWEET POTATO FRITTERS

**8 cups (2 L) grated sweet potatoes (or a mix of
    potatoes, yams, and sweet potatoes)**
2 garlic cloves, minced
1 cup (250 mL) rice flour
2 tsp salt
¼ tsp cayenne pepper
⅛ tsp garam masala (p. 210)
¼ cup (60 mL) soy milk
1 tsp apple cider vinegar
2 tbsp grapeseed oil
¼ cup (60 mL) chopped fresh cilantro
⅓ cup (80 mL) chopped green onions
grapeseed oil, for frying

In a large bowl, mix all ingredients with a wooden spoon
until well incorporated. Use your hands, if needed, to
combine ingredients.

Preheat and generously oil a frying pan or griddle on
medium. Use ¼ cup (60 mL) batter to form patties or
fritters about ½-in (1-cm) thick. Fry on each side for 5
minutes. Serve immediately.

Makes about 18 fritters.

ROASTED PINEAPPLE

1 whole pineapple, chopped into chunks
1 tbsp coconut oil, melted
¼–½ tsp red pepper flakes, to taste
1 tsp tamari
1 tbsp lime juice

Preheat oven to 350°F (180°C).
In a bowl, toss pineapple with coconut oil, red pepper
flakes, tamari, and lime juice. On an unoiled cookie
sheet, roast pineapple for 15 minutes, turn chunks over
then roast for another 15 minutes.

TO PLATE:

Apple Tamarind Chutney (p. 196)
Smoke-Cured Coconut (p. 210)
Coconut Sour Cream (p. 195)
fresh cilantro, chopped, for garnish

In middle of a plate, spread 3 tbsp chutney. Place 1 fritter
on each side of chutney. Top with pineapple chunks and a
sprinkle of Smoke-Cured Coconut. Spoon 1 tbsp Coconut
Sour Cream on side. Garnish with 1 tsp fresh cilantro.

PEANUT BUTTER OAT WAFFLES WITH WHITE CHOCOLATE MOUSSE & VANILLA PLUM COMPOTE

An oh-so-fancy take on a peanut butter and jelly sandwich that makes one sweet, sweet breakfast!

• **MAKES 8–10 WAFFLES.**

WHITE CHOCOLATE MOUSSE

¼ cup (60 mL) coconut oil
¼ cup (60 mL) chopped cocoa butter
1 cup (250 mL) coconut milk
¼ cup (60 mL) maple syrup
1 vanilla bean, scraped

In a heat-proof bowl on boiling water or in a double boiler, melt coconut oil and cocoa butter. In a blender or food processor, combine coconut milk, maple syrup, and vanilla bean. While blender is running, slowly pour melted coconut oil and cocoa butter into blender and blend until well-incorporated and smooth. Pour into a bowl or container, cover, and chill overnight in refrigerator.

Makes 2½ cups (625 mL).

VANILLA PLUM COMPOTE

1½ cups (375 mL) pitted and quartered purple Italian plums
½ vanilla bean (a shelled bean works great)
¼ cup (60 mL) brown rice syrup
2–3 tbsp dark brown sugar

In a pot on medium heat, combine all ingredients and bring to a simmer, stirring constantly. When plums begin to soften and cook down, adjust brown sugar, to taste. Let simmer for 10 minutes, until thick. Set aside to cool. (Keeps for 3–4 weeks in refrigerator.)

Makes 1 cup (250 mL).

PEANUT BUTTER OAT WAFFLES

1½ cups (375 mL) flour
⅔ cup (160 mL) whole oats
1 tbsp cocoa powder (optional)
½ tsp baking powder
½ tsp baking soda
¼ tsp salt
1½ cups (375 mL) milk of your choice
**   (nut, rice, etc.)**
½ cup (125 mL) natural peanut butter
3 tbsp maple syrup
3 tbsp oil
1 tsp apple cider vinegar
1 tsp vanilla extract

In a bowl, mix together dry ingredients and make a well. In a separate bowl, whisk together wet ingredients. Make sure peanut butter is well-incorporated. Pour wet ingredients into dry and combine gently until just mixed.

Preheat waffle iron or waffle maker and follow manufacturer's instructions. Oil iron lightly.

TO PLATE:

Place 1 or 2 waffles on a plate and top with Vanilla Plum Compote and White Chocolate Mousse.

PUMPKIN WAFFLES

The first waffle brunch VSS served was on a snowy morning in Vancouver, which is really rare and special. On that memorable morning, these waffles were paired with Vanilla Cashew Cream (p. 135) and Ginger-Infused Maple Syrup (p. 202).

• MAKES 10–12 WAFFLES.

1 tbsp ground flax seeds
3 tbsp water
2 cups (250 mL) flour
2 tsp baking powder
1 tsp baking soda
2 tsp ground cinnamon
½ tsp ground nutmeg
⅛ tsp ground cloves
½ tsp salt
1⅔ cups (395 mL) milk of your choice (nut, rice, etc.)
⅔ cup (160 mL) pumpkin purée (or mashed yams)
3 tbsp maple syrup
3 tbsp grapeseed oil
1 tbsp apple cider vinegar

In a bowl, whisk together ground flax seeds and water and set aside.

In a separate bowl, combine dry ingredients and make a well. In another bowl, whisk milk, purée, maple syrup, oil, and vinegar. Add flax-water mix to wet ingredients. Pour wet ingredients into dry and combine gently until just mixed.

Preheat waffle iron or waffle maker and follow manufacturer's instructions. Oil iron lightly.

DOUBLE CHOCOLATE WAFFLES WITH MOCHA CREAM

I like to serve these waffles with Raspberry Maple Syrup and fresh berries.

• **MAKES 8–10 WAFFLES.**

MOCHA CREAM

1 cup (250 mL) coconut cream
¼ cup (60 mL) coconut oil
¼ cup (60 mL) brown rice syrup
1 tbsp maple syrup
1 tbsp instant coffee
2 tbsp cocoa powder
1 tsp vanilla extract

In a pot on medium heat, whisk all ingredients together until coffee dissolves and oil melts. In a blender or food processor, purée until smooth. Pour into bowl or container, cover, and chill overnight in refrigerator.

Makes 1½ cups (375 mL).

DOUBLE CHOCOLATE WAFFLES

2 cups (500 mL) flour
¼ cup (60 mL) cocoa powder
1 tsp baking powder
1 tsp baking soda
½ tsp salt
⅛ tsp ground cloves
2 cups milk of your choice (nut, rice, etc.)
3 tbsp grapeseed oil
3 tbsp maple syrup
1 tsp apple cider vinegar
1 tsp vanilla extract

1 banana, mashed
8 Medjool dates, chopped
⅔ cup (160 mL) chocolate chips or chopped chocolate

In a bowl, mix dry ingredients together and make a well. In a separate bowl, whisk together wet ingredients, then stir in mashed banana and dates. Add chocolate chips. Pour wet ingredients into dry and combine gently until just mixed.

Preheat waffle iron or waffle maker and follow manufacturer's instructions. Oil iron lightly.

TO PLATE:

Raspberry Maple Syrup (p. 203)

Top each waffle with Mocha Cream, a drizzle of Raspberry Maple Syrup, and fresh berries.

TEAS & SODAS

- ROOIBOS CHAI
- TOASTED COCONUT GREEN TEA
- LAVENDER BLACK TEA
- GINGER BEER SYRUP
- LAVENDER LIME SODA CONCENTRATE
- ROOT BEER CHICORY SODA CONCENTRATE

ROOIBOS CHAI

Rooibos is my favorite herbal tea. It is low in tannins, so it doesn't become bitter, and is full of antioxidants.

• **MAKES 2½ CUPS (625 ML).**

1 tbsp whole cloves
1 tsp whole black peppercorns
1 star anise
1 tsp whole cardamom pods
¼ cup (60 mL) crushed cinnamon sticks
⅓ cup (80 mL) dried chopped ginger
2 cups (500 mL) brewed rooibos tea
1 tsp allspice

In a food processor, or with a mortar and pestle, grind cloves, peppercorns, star anise, and cardamom. In a bowl, combine ground spices with crushed cinnamon sticks, ginger, brewed tea, and allspice. Store in a sealed jar in refrigerator. Use 2 tsp of tea for each cup (250 mL) water or milk of your choice. Steep for as long as desired.

TOASTED COCONUT GREEN TEA

This tea has an amazing toasted flavor.

• **MAKES ABOUT ¾ CUP (185 ML).**

½ cup (125 mL) Sencha green tea
⅓ cup (80 mL) toasted unsweetened coconut

Combine tea and coconut and store in a sealed jar. Use 1 tsp for each cup (250 mL) hot water. Steep for 2–5 minutes.

Rooibos Chai, 181

Toasted Coconut Green Tea, 181

LAVENDER BLACK TEA

Reminiscent of Earl Grey.

• **MAKES ⅔ CUP (160 ML).**

½ cup (125 mL) loose black tea
2 tbsp dried lavender flowers
2 tsp chopped dried orange peel

Combine all ingredients and store in a sealed jar. Use 1 tsp for each cup (250 mL) hot water. Steep for 2–4 minutes.

GINGER BEER SYRUP

Extra spicy.

• **MAKES 1⅔ CUPS (630 ML).**

1 cup (250 mL) thinly sliced ginger
1 cup (250 mL) water
¾ cup (185 mL) maple syrup or agave nectar
¼ cup (60 mL) lime juice

In a pot on medium-high heat, combine all ingredients except lime juice. Bring to a boil and simmer for 25 minutes. Let syrup sit overnight before straining. Add lime juice. To make Ginger Beer, use up to 2 tbsp concentrate per 8 oz (230 g) sparkling water.

LAVENDER LIME SODA CONCENTRATE

Refreshing, with a subtle hint of lavender.

• **MAKES 1½ CUPS (625 ML).**

¾ cup (185 mL) agave nectar
½ cup (125 mL) lime juice
2 tbsp dried lavender flowers

In a pot on medium-high heat, bring agave nectar and lime juice to a boil. Boil for 6 minutes. Remove from heat. Add lavender and let steep for 20 minutes. Strain. To make soda, use 1 tbsp concentrate per 8 oz (230 g) sparkling water.

ROOT BEER CHICORY SODA CONCENTRATE

An herbal root beer.

• **MAKES 2½ CUPS (625 ML) CONCENTRATE.**

½ cup (125 mL) maple syrup
½ cup (125 mL) agave nectar
1½ cups (375 mL) water
1 tbsp thinly sliced fresh ginger
1 vanilla bean, scraped
1 cinnamon stick
1 star anise
1 tsp licorice root (licorice tea bag works well)
3 tbsp roasted chicory root

In a pot on medium-high heat, combine all ingredients except for chicory. Bring to a boil, reduce heat, and simmer for 15 minutes. Add chicory and simmer for another 10 minutes. Remove from heat and let cool before straining. To make soda, use 2 tbsp concentrate per 8 oz (230 g) sparkling water.

VSS PANTRY

- ROASTED GARLIC
- SMOKY BALSAMIC MARINADE FOR PORTOBELLO MUSHROOMS
- MISO SESAME SHIITAKE MUSHROOMS
- REJUVELAC NUT CHEESE
- CASHEW CHEESE
- COCONUT CASHEW CHEESE
- PINE NUT PARMESAN
- MISO CASHEW CHEESE
- COCONUT MELTING CHEESE
- SESAME WALNUT PARMESAN
- COCONUT SOUR CREAM
- CARROT TAMARIND CHUTNEY
- APPLE TAMARIND CHUTNEY
- FRESH PEACH CHUTNEY
- APPLE CHIPOTLE LIME CHUTNEY

- QUICK PICKLED BEETS
- QUICK PICKLED SPICY STRING BEANS
- BALSAMIC MAPLE PECANS
- SALTED MAPLE PISTACHIOS
- ANISE-TOASTED SUNFLOWER SEEDS
- GINGER-INFUSED MAPLE SYRUP
- SPICED MAPLE SYRUP
- RASPBERRY MAPLE SYRUP
- APPLE REDUCTION
- CHIPOTLE APPLE REDUCTION
- BALSAMIC REDUCTION
- ROSEMARY OLIVE OIL
- SMOKE-INFUSED OLIVE OIL
- SMOKE-CURED COCONUT
- GARAM MASALA
- GOMASHIO

ROASTED GARLIC

Roasted garlic is used a lot in this book. Here's how I do it.

1 whole garlic bulb
1–3 tbsp olive oil

Preheat oven or toaster oven to 350°F (180°C).

Cut top off garlic bulb so that cloves are exposed. Place bulb in aluminum foil and form foil into a small bowl.

Pour in olive oil and wrap foil into a sealed packet. Set packet in a small oven-proof bowl and bake for 25 minutes, or until garlic is soft and fragrant.

SMOKY BALSAMIC MARINADE FOR PORTOBELLO MUSHROOMS

A great marinade for roasted, dehydrated, or pan-fried mushrooms.

• MAKES ENOUGH FOR 4–8 PORTOBELLOS.

2 tbsp balsamic vinegar
1 tbsp olive oil
2 garlic cloves, smashed with the side of a knife
1 tsp maple syrup
1 tsp tamari
½ tsp liquid smoke
½ tsp Dijon mustard
1 sprig rosemary
½ tsp salt
½ tsp pepper
¼ tsp crushed red pepper flakes
4–8 portobello mushrooms

In a bowl, whisk all ingredients together, except mushrooms. Add sliced or whole portobellos. Cover and let marinate for 30 minutes–2 hours in refrigerator. You can also marinate mushrooms a in a resealable plastic bag.

MISO SESAME SHIITAKE MUSHROOMS

These flavorful mushrooms are a great addition to most salads or for simply tossing with soba noodles.

1 tbsp toasted sesame seeds
1 tsp water
1 tsp toasted sesame oil
1 tsp olive oil
1 tsp brown rice vinegar
½ tsp Dijon mustard
1 tsp miso
½ tsp tamari
¼ tsp liquid smoke (optional)
⅛ tsp cayenne pepper
4–10 shiitake mushrooms, depending on size, sliced

In a bowl, whisk all ingredients except shiitakes together. Add shiitakes, cover, and let sit for 30 minutes–2 hours in refrigerator. You can also put mushrooms and marinade in a resealable plastic bag to marinate.

If you have a dehydrator, place shiitakes on screen and dehydrate for about 1 hour, checking often, until mushrooms have softened.

Or, preheat oven to 350°F (180°C). Place mushrooms on lightly oiled baking pan and roast for 5–7 minutes, turn over, and roast for another 5–7 minutes.

Or, pan-fry shiitakes in a non-stick or lightly oiled pan on medium-high heat for 2–3 minutes on each side.

REJUVELAC NUT CHEESE

Fermented nut cheeses are popular not only for their health benefits (they're a great source of vitamin B12) but also their amazingly complex, cheesy flavor. Although fermentation takes time, it also adds beneficial probiotics to the cheese.

• **MAKES 1½ CUPS (375 ML).**

⅓ cup (80 mL) organic wheat berries
8 cups (2 L) filtered distilled water
1 cup (250 mL) raw nuts (cashews, pine nuts, or
   macadamia nuts)

In a 4-cup (1-L) glass jar, soak wheat berries for 12 hours in 1 cup (250 mL) water.

Using a strainer, strain berries and return to jar. Cover top of jar with a clean dish towel or paper towel and seal with rubber band. Leave in a warm, sunny spot for 36 hours. Rinse berries with 1 cup filtered water every 12 hours.

After 36 hours, or when berries begin to sprout slightly, rinse them a final time and fill jar with 3 cups (750 mL) filtered water. Place fresh dish towel or new paper towel over jar and set in a warm, dark spot. Check every 12 hours for signs of fermentation: the rejuvelac should appear slightly cloudy and bubbly and should have a fermented "cheesy" fragrance. This will take about 2 days. If mixture start to smell vinegary or sour, throw it out.

When rejuvelac is ready, strain out berries and reserve liquid. Pour it back into jar and seal with a lid. Rejuvelac will keep in refrigerator for up to 1 week.

To ferment nuts, bring rejuvelac to room temperature, add nuts, cover top of jar with paper towel, and let sit in a warm, dark place for 12 hours. Strain rejuvelac and reserve liquid. Use nuts as suggested in Cashew Cheese (p. 192).

CASHEW CHEESE

Cashews are my favorite nut to use when making fermented cheese, both for their fat content and subtle flavor, but macadamia nuts, walnuts, hazelnuts, and almonds also make tasty cheeses.

• **MAKES 1 ½ CUPS (375 ML).**

1 cup (250 mL) raw cashews, soaked in 1 cup rejuvelac (p. 191) for 12 hours, strained, soaking liquid reserved
1 tbsp lemon juice
½–1 tsp sea salt

In a blender or food processor, blend cashews with lemon juice, salt, and just enough soaking liquid to facilitate blending, up to ⅓ cup (80 mL). Blend until smooth. Store in a sealed container in refrigerator for up to 2 weeks.

HERBED CHEESE VARIATION:

½ tsp freshly ground black pepper
¼ tsp red pepper flakes
½ tsp each fresh chopped herbs of your choice (e.g., rosemary and sage, thyme and lavender, or basil)

Stir herbs into blended cheese.

COCONUT CASHEW CHEESE

This is a less spreadable cheese with a more saucy consistency than Cashew Cheese. Its gentle flavor reminds me a little of cottage cheese. It goes nicely with Yam & Walnut Croquettes (p. 91) or Crêpes (p. 171) paired with your favorite fruit preserves.

• **MAKES 2 CUPS (500 ML).**

1 cup (250 mL) raw cashews, soaked in 1 cup rejuvelac for 12 hours, strained, soaking liquid reserved
1 tbsp lemon juice
1 tsp sea salt
2 tsp apple cider vinegar
¼ cup (60 mL) coconut milk
2 tbsp rejuvelac soaking liquid (p. 191)

In a blender or food processor, purée cashews with lemon juice, salt, apple cider vinegar, coconut milk, and rejuvelac until smooth. Store in a sealed container in refrigerator for up to 2 weeks.

PINE NUT PARMESAN

Crumble this vegan cheese over salads, popcorn, and pasta. Or omit the dehydrating step and add it to pesto.

• **MAKES ABOUT 1 CUP (250 ML).**

**1 cup (250 mL) raw pine nuts, soaked in 1 cup
rejuvelac for 12 hours, strained, soaking
liquid reserved**
1 tbsp lemon juice
1¼ tsp sea salt

In a blender or food processor, blend pine nuts with lemon juice, salt, and just enough soaking liquid to facilitate blending, up to ⅓ cup (80 mL). Blend until smooth.

On a Silpat (non-stick) dehydrator tray, spread mixture in a thin layer ⅛-in (3-mm) thick. Dehydrate at 115°F (46°C) for 4 hours, or until cheese is crisp and crumbles nicely. Store in a sealed container at room temperature.

MISO CASHEW CHEESE

This nut cheese is made by soaking the nuts overnight, which is less time-consuming than the method using rejuvelac. The texture is the same as the fermented cheese (p. 192).

• **MAKES 1½ CUPS (375 ML).**

1 tbsp unpasteurized miso
2 cups (500 mL) water
1 cup (250 mL) raw cashews
1 tbsp lemon juice
2 tsp tahini
1 tbsp nutritional yeast
1 tsp apple cider vinegar
½–1 tsp salt, to taste

In a bowl, whisk miso into water. Add cashews and soak for 12 hours. Drain cashews, reserving ⅓ cup (80 mL) soaking liquid. In a blender or food processor, add cashews and remainder of ingredients and blend until smooth. Adjust salt to taste. Store in a sealed container in the refrigerator for up to 2 weeks.

COCONUT MELTING CHEESE

A perfect cheese sauce for broiling on toast, nachos, and pizza.

• **MAKES ¾ CUP (185 ML).**

6 roasted garlic cloves (p. 189), skins removed
1 tsp tahini
½ cup (125 mL) soy or almond milk
2 tbsp coconut oil, melted
1 tbsp nutritional yeast
1 tsp tomato paste
½ tsp Dijon mustard
2 tsp fine corn flour
2 tsp lemon juice
1 tsp salt

In a blender or food processor, blend all ingredients until smooth.

SESAME WALNUT PARMESAN

A great-tasting cheese to sprinkle over pizza, pasta, salads, and soups.

• **MAKES ½ CUP (125 ML).**

2 garlic cloves
⅓ cup (80 mL) walnuts
2 tbsp sesame seeds
⅓ cup (80 mL) nutritional yeast
½ tsp salt
¼ tsp red pepper flakes

In a blender or food processor, pulse all ingredients until crumbly and evenly blended. Store in a sealed container in the refrigerator.

COCONUT SOUR CREAM

This is the recipe I use the most—it goes with anything!

• **MAKES 2 CUPS (500 ML).**

1 13-oz (370-g) can coconut cream
1 tbsp lemon juice
1 tsp apple cider vinegar
1 tbsp tahini
¼ tsp salt
1½ tsp brown rice syrup
¼ cup (60 mL) plain non-dairy yogurt (optional)

In a blender or food processor, blend all ingredients until smooth. Refrigerate overnight to thicken.

CARROT TAMARIND CHUTNEY

This spicy chutney is nicely complemented by the sweetness of the carrots.

• MAKES 2 CUPS (500 ML).

1 tbsp refined coconut oil
1 medium onion, chopped
½ tsp salt
3 garlic cloves, smashed
½ habañero pepper, seeded and chopped, or 1 tbsp habañero or Scotch bonnet hot sauce
2 medium carrots, chopped
3 tbsp tamarind paste/concentrate
1 tbsp agave nectar
¾ cup (185 mL) stock (p. 45)

In a medium pot on medium heat, melt coconut oil. Add onions and salt and cook until onions are translucent. Add garlic, habañero peppers, and carrots and cook for another 2 minutes, until carrots are softened. Add tamarind, agave, and stock and bring to a boil. Reduce heat and simmer for another 10 minutes. Remove from heat.

In a food processor or blender, blend all ingredients until smooth. Be careful when blending hot liquids. Store in a well-sealed glass container in the refrigerator for up to 2 weeks.

APPLE TAMARIND CHUTNEY

This chutney is tangy and sweet and pairs well with Sweet Potato Fritters (p. 172).

• MAKES 4 CUPS (1 L).

8 oz (230 g) whole tamarind or ½ cup (125 mL) tamarind paste/concentrate
1 tsp grapeseed oil
½ cup (125 mL) chopped shallots or red onions
2 apples, cored and chopped (Granny Smith is best)
1 tsp red pepper flakes
½ tsp cumin
1 tbsp tamari
½ cup (125 mL) maple syrup
2 cups (500 mL) water

If using whole tamarind, which comes in a condensed brick, soak in ½ cup (125 mL) boiling water for 10 minutes and strain out seeds before adding to recipe.

In a medium pot on medium-high, heat oil. Add shallots and sauté until translucent. Add apples, red pepper flakes, and cumin and cook for another 2 minutes, stirring constantly. Add tamarind, tamari, maple syrup, and water and let simmer for 15 minutes. Remove from heat.

In a blender or food processor, or with an immersion blender, blend chutney until smooth. Be careful when blending hot liquids.

Pour into jars while hot and process in a water bath if you are planning to store the chutney long-term. Unprocessed, it will keep in a well-sealed glass container in the refrigerator for up to 2 weeks.

FRESH PEACH CHUTNEY

Every August I go up to the Okanagan valley, the fruit-growing region in the Interior of British Columbia, and bring back fresh, ripe peaches. This chutney is a little spicy, and is great with roasted cauliflower or Baked Eggplant Samosas (p. 27).

• MAKES 6 CUPS (1.5 ML).

2 tbsp coconut oil
1 medium shallot, finely chopped
2–4 fresh Thai chili peppers (depending on how spicy you like it), finely chopped
1 tbsp grated fresh ginger
⅛ tsp garam masala (p. 210)
2 lbs (1 kg) peaches (approximately 10), peeled and cubed
1 tsp tamari
¼ cup (60 mL) lime juice
⅓–½ cup (80–125 mL) vinegar
⅓ cup (80 mL) brown rice syrup (to taste)
⅓ cup (80 mL) chopped fresh cilantro

In a large pot on medium-high heat, melt coconut oil. Add shallots, chilies, ginger, and garam masala and sauté until shallots are translucent. Add peaches, tamari, lime juice, vinegar, and brown rice syrup. Simmer for 10 minutes. Stir in cilantro just before removing from heat.

Pour into jars while hot and process in a water bath if you are planning to store the chutney long-term. If not processing, store in a sealed glass container in the refrigerator for up to 2 weeks.

APPLE CHIPOTLE LIME CHUTNEY

Spicy, sweet, and smoky, this chutney pairs well with fresh corn on the cob, fritters, and cornbread. For chipotle peppers I usually take a whole can in adobo sauce, blend it in the food processor, and keep it in the refrigerator for up to 4 weeks.

• MAKES 2 CUPS (500 ML).

2 apples, peeled and finely chopped
3 tbsp unsweetened apple sauce
1 tbsp blended chipotle peppers, in adobo sauce
1 lime, juiced and zested
1 ½ tsp lime juice
¼ cup (60 mL) agave nectar
¾ cup (185 mL) water
¼ cup (60 mL) water
1 tsp cornstarch

In a pot on medium heat, combine all ingredients except ¼ cup (60 mL) water and cornstarch. Bring to a boil, then reduce heat, and simmer on low.

Meanwhile, in a small bowl, whisk cornstarch into ¼ cup water. Whisk into chutney once it simmers, and cook for 10 minutes. Remove from heat.

Pour into jars while hot and process in a water bath if you are planning to store the chutney long-term. If not processing, will keep in a sealed glass container in the refrigerator for up to 2 weeks.